Humanity's Guidebook to Ascension

Channeled Guidance to Prepare for
the 5ʰ Dimension and Beyond

SARAH A'RYANA

Design, Photography and Cover by Tartaruga Feliz
Edited by Marissa Young

To find more about Sarah A'ryana visit saraharyana.com

Book One

This book is dedicated to Humanity and our Awakening.

The veil is lifting and together we rise,

to

Love,

Unity

&

Peace.

We are moving into a higher dimension.

We are returning to the love of self,

loving one another

and

our magnificent planet.

The time is now dear ones.

Contents

HUMANITY'S GUIDEBOOK TO ASCENSION

*Channeled Guidance to Prepare for
the 5ᵗʰ Dimension and Beyond*

PREFACE

Greetings,

We are the Divine Light Collective and we are honored to help humanity at this time. We are a Collective Group of Light Beings: The Ascended Masters of the Divine Feminine and the Divine Masculine, Galactic Masters of the Light, and Members of the Multiverse Light Councils.

We offer guidance to all, as humanity moves through these times of Ascension.

Sarah is our channeler and we are honored to have her gift of Divine Light Service. Sarah has lived many lifetimes on Mother Earth as a healer, seer, oracle, leader for the soft-spoken and forgotten. She is a Rising Phoenix, a Divine Light Channeler, a Holder of the Light, and Gatekeeper of the Wisdom Keepers.

There will be a series of three books. We recommend reading them in order and following the steps provided to give you the maximum assistance and growth at this time.

Book One is a guidebook to help humanity move through this shift of Grand Awakening. The next few years will be an intense time of change and dismantlement of all systems and constructs on Earth.

To welcome the new world, the old paradigm must fall. With this change, humanity will shift into an enlightened state of being. One of equality, strength, and compassion.

It is our honor to share this simple yet profound wisdom of the Ancients with you.

A word of caution to the reader: Book one will awaken parts of you that can lead to Dark Nights of the Soul. Take the time to process and integrate the awakenings that can occur, by honoring your body with rest and self-care.

Please note: Some words are capitalized in this book such as Soul, Light, Love, and Being. This is to emphasize the word's higher frequency and vibration.

INTRODUCTION

Let's go back to the beginning...

SOURCE

Source holds many titles and meanings. On Earth, humans have called Source: God, Allah, Jehovah, Christ, the Divine, the Creator, the Almighty, and much more.

All creation is derived from Source.

Source is a consciousness of pure Divine Love and Light.

Each of you is from Source. We are all created from the same place of origin.

In the beginning, Source sent out waves of Souls to create various worlds; to explore and experience duality, to love and live in many different forms.

It is not an easy task for the Soul to leave Source in this way. Once you have left the ocean consciousness state of Love, each Soul wants to return to that feeling at its purest form. It is understood that each Soul is to partake in its own growth and experiences. A Soul never truly leaves Source.

Each Soul is an entity within itself. The Soul, your

Multidimensional Highest Self can experience many aspects in many different realities at the same time. For example, there can be twelve expressions of you in other forms and planets, existing all at once.

Each aspect will have a different personality and can reside in another physical form. Once that life comes to an end, your energy connects back with your Soul, your Highest Self.

When this transition occurs, some Souls will be immediately placed into an incubation vessel for healing. It depends on the trauma they have experienced in their lifetime. Other Souls will be moved into a life review process and decide on their mission and growth for their next lifetime.

In the beginning, the groups which first came from Source created worlds, dimensions, and universes. Universes within universes formed and each Soul experienced the depths of polarity within those realms. There was the realization that to experience polarity and the range of feelings and emotions, the Soul would go through levels of dimensions that hold the frequency for those experiences to be felt.

Within these experiences, wars were created. Galactic wars, similar to what you see in the science fiction movies on Earth. To experience duality, both darkness and Light are needed.

Beings began to stray as the corruption of greed and

power took over.

This led to destruction and created karma and trauma on many planets. When the imbalance on a planet reached the point of not being able to move forward, a decision had to be made.

This decision was made by a Light council within that realm. It is not a decision to take lightly. If the decision is to continue on the planet, reinforcements can be brought in to help shift the planet and create an awakening. Giving the Souls that live there an opportunity to balance the karma and trauma in that realm. The decision can also be made for that planet to be destroyed to begin anew. This decision weighs heavily on each Soul who makes this final decision.

One of the groups of Beings who were fighting in the wars began to travel from planet to planet, creating fear and control amongst the species. Their goal or objective was to take over each planet. Stripping the planet of its natural resources and killing or controlling the species that were living there into submission.

These Beings feed off of others' energy such as their gifts and their Light. They have created an intensive, false matrix in this realm and have been on Earth for many centuries. They created a system to enslave humanity into a controlled 3D reality.

Everything from music, food, media, TV, news, movies, governments, religion, health care, and education are designed to keep humans at a certain level of submission.

Let us be clear: even within the highest of vibrations and realms, there can be fallen Light Beings, Entities, Angels, and Archangels. There have been many stories created on Earth about Fallen Angels, Gods and Goddesses, Lemuria, Atlantis, Egypt, King Arthur, Jesus, Mary Magdalene and so many more. Each story that was written has a sliver of truth to it, however, falsehoods have been told to bring the dark to the lightest of stories and Souls.

Each Soul is here to have experiences. The belief that one will go to "Hell" is one of the controlling ways to entrap humans.

There is a much bigger picture unfolding with what is occurring on Earth. The Fallen ones are controlling the Earth with released Reptilians, Draconian and other species that were imprisoned on other planets. The Fallen Ones released them to bring havoc and control to your world.

When Earth was created, it was all an experiment. It took millions of years to begin the process of seeding the planet with cells to then coagulate and fuse with other cells. Once this process had begun, it was a natural evolution that began to take over.

The original humans on this planet were the neanderthals. The neanderthals survived the elements and had little brain power until Beings from other galaxies began experimenting with their DNA. Some of these Beings settled on Earth and merged the two species together.

This began another evolution of the human. The human would then move into a journey of thousands of years to get to the point of equal balance for the highest potential of its kind and this is what is coming forward now.

The original plan on Earth was to create a species to become the peacemakers for the Galactic Wars. Twelve enlightened species from other universes donated a part of their DNA to create human beings.

However, there is also another truth: many who were in the Galactic Wars wanted to create humans to become slaves so they could help them in the Galactic Wars and as a result, they would feed off their energy.

This is happening now to many Souls. Beings are attached to some Souls and these Souls are being used and trapped against their will. We bring this to your attention not to create fear but to create awareness. The time is now for each Soul to take responsibility for their energy and to listen to what is inside of you and your heart-wise intuition.

Many Beings that created Earth have seen their ways through fighting in the Galactic Wars and have returned to correct the past by coming through as Lightworkers. These Lightworkers have come to Earth now, experiencing what they had birthed, the veil of illusion and amnesia, thus becoming a slave to the systems in place until their awakening. Many of these Lightworkers have experienced many lifetimes on Earth trying to help humanity. In the present moment, the energy has shifted and will move ahead, transcending the majority of humans into the New Earth.

The Beings currently in power will now shift and be released from planet Earth. All truths will come forward and the veil of forgetfulness will be lifted once and for all. The vibration which the Earth is now experiencing cannot sustain the ones that are in power any longer. They cannot be in this frequency, as the illusion exposes all to see.

Many of you may recall there was a prophecy in the year 2012 that it was going to be the end of times in the Mayan Calendar. And yes, that was a possible outcome. However, with the number of Lightworkers that had been awoken by that time, there was enough Light to shift the timeline, to what is now being called the Golden Age.

WHAT IS THE GOLDEN AGE?

It is the time when all blinders come off and each Soul moves into its power and spiritual strength.

The Golden Age brings the downfall of the Fallen Ones: the ones who have been in control along with the

Reptilians, Draconian, and other species to help enslave humans. What is occurring now is very similar to Atlantis.

Atlantis also had Fallen Ones that created a time of experimentation and hierarchy to feed off of others' Light.

We want humanity to understand that the Fallen Ones that have been controlling Earth are not necessarily evil. They are originally from the Light and they are humans that have been led astray down a dark and shadowy road. This is not to say there will not be repercussions, as there is ownership each Soul takes on with each experience they have. Once the dust settles, there will be a welcoming of the dark energies and both sides will unite together as one.

When a Soul transitions and goes over their life review, all experiences that the Soul has done to others are felt in their Being. Many Souls go through an incubation of healing to be able to go through their life review process with a greater awareness of consciousness.

We would like each Soul to know, not all Souls have been "perfect" in their experiences. There is no such thing as living a life without the dark in the 3rd dimension. For with Light there is always dark. Each side holds an experience that is neither good nor bad. Each Soul has done what humans perceive as dishonorable intentions through their lifetimes. This could be causing harm to other humans or species through violence, either physically, mentally, or emotionally. This could be playing a role in harming themselves, other planets, or animals. This is the shadow side of oneself.

It is through awareness, experience, and Love that a Being experiences the many levels of the Soul.

In the coming months, we recommend each Soul use their discernment. The human standing in front of you, which you perceive to be "human", may not be all that is shown to you. All Souls at some point in their past lives have been other species than human beings. Some Beings who are here at this moment have experienced life as a human many times, as they heard the call for help from Earth with great urgency. We want each Soul to be aware of the hidden agendas of other species who have a human vessel as their disguise.

This information was created to bring awareness to each one of you. To follow your intuition and the signals your body is giving you. We will go into greater detail about the signs and symptoms of how your body reacts to these circumstances in the chapters ahead.

Through the cycles on Earth, there have been many lifetimes where there was peace on Mother Earth. Plants, animals, trees, humans, and other species were living here in harmony. There was a deep knowing that Mother Earth is a living Being and All is One. When someone needed to kill an animal to eat for survival, there was deep gratitude and reverence for its sacrifices and the life-giving energy was balanced.

Humans were aware of how powerful the mind can be and maintained thoughts of Love, positivity, joy, and Light.

Before you came to Earth, in your Divine Essence, your Multidimensional Self and your Team of Light (Light Beings and Guides) decided on what experiences you wanted to learn and grow from. You chose your family, the place you were born, and the time when you would enter and exit Mother Earth.

Since 2012, there has been a HUGE shift in the awakening of humanity. Drastic changes began in the year 2020 and will continue for the next decade. There are currently Legions of Light Beings surrounding Mother Earth assisting her and her inhabitants in ascending to the next dimension.

This first book is to provide you with the tools to help YOU at this moment. To help YOU shift into joy, Light, and expansion, rediscovering your gifts as a Soul.

Our goal and purpose are to help you move through the depths of sorrow and unhappiness, shifting your awareness to the beautiful Being of Light that you are. You can do anything. You can create the reality you want. You can be happy and filled with joy.

The key to transitioning into your gifts at this time is through awareness of your thoughts, movement in your body, and Self Love for oneself.

PART 1

HEALING THE BODY

AND MIND

The following 10 steps provide you with optimal health to help heal the body and mind out of the 3D illusion. We recommend reading through all 10 steps and then going back and selecting what resonates with you. Ultimately, the goal is to have all the steps be a part of your daily life for maximum healing before moving into parts two and three of this book.

STEP 1: POSITIVE AFFIRMATIONS

How many thoughts go through one's mind in a day? Millions!

You have the ability to bring awareness to your thoughts and make every single one of them positive, filled with Love and Light.

Positive Affirmations are the first step to refocusing your thoughts.

Write down positive affirmations and place them all around where you live, at eye level. We recommend avoiding words such as: no, never, can't, but and such.

Here are a few examples of positive affirmations:

I am at peace.

I am calm.

I am Light.

I am relaxed.

All is well.

I am Love.

I am filled with joy.

I am in a strong, healthy body.

I am in a loving relationship, we treat each other with respect and Love.

I am in a job that I enjoy and I am compensated well.

I Love myself unconditionally.

I Love Mother Earth and all of her plants, animals, trees, crystals and minerals.

I have a Soul tribe of friends that love me for who I am and love me unconditionally.

I am filled with joy and happiness.

I am grateful for my life and this opportunity on Mother Earth to expand my Soul.

I am grateful for my Team of Light as they guide me and help me on my journey.

I am grateful for the communication within my body as it provides me with the information and knowledge to keep me healthy.

These affirmations help shift the mind as you observe these powerful statements all around you. You are not focusing on how this will happen. These affirmations are what you truly desire in your heart. With this exercise, take a moment to think about what you want to attract in your life and how you want to feel. When creating each affirmation, *sit with it, feel it and visualize it.*

Once you feel you have embodied your affirmation and it is no longer needed, remove it and create a new one that is meaningful and important to you in the present moment. There is no time frame on how long your affirmations need to be relevant, as this is an individual experience. You will know when the time is right to change your affirmations or move on to the next step.

When you arrive on Mother Earth, you enter through the veil of forgetting who you are. The ego and victim come into play as you live out your life, casting doubt, fear, and anxiety into the Soul. This is part of the entrapment in this illusion.

To move through these experiences, it is important to balance the ego and leave the victim role behind, as this will help you break through the veil. To do so, you must bring awareness to your everyday thoughts.

STEP 2: THE PAUSE METHOD

Bring awareness to your mind through the *Pause method*. This method shows you how powerful you can be. Every time a thought comes into your mind that's negative, we recommend using the Pause Method.

The Pause Method

When a negative thought comes into the mind, immediately say "*Pause*" in your mind and *replace the thought with a positive one and repeat the positive thought 3 times.*

A few examples of negative thought patterns are:

I'm not good enough, I'm ugly, I'm fat, I'm unsuccessful, I'm a failure, there's not enough time, there's too much to do, I'm a bad parent, spouse, friend, sibling, no one likes me, and so on.

Here are some examples of positive thoughts:

I am good enough, I *feel* good today, *I am* doing a good job, *there is* enough time, *it will* all work out, *all* is well, *I am* a good spouse, sibling, parent, daughter, son, friend, and so on.

When you are committed and follow through with the Pause Method *every day*, you will begin to see the results. This process takes a few months and you will be amazed at what happens to the mind as it shifts into a more positive outlook on life.

In the beginning, it can be a struggle, as the ego feels under attack and will begin to produce more negative thoughts. Halfway through this exercise, you will notice you don't need to use the Pause Method as often.

Eventually, the ego will be in a more balanced state and you will now have a cheerleader on your side. This cheerleader is your Higher Self, cheering you on every step of the way.

For example, if you're feeling overwhelmed from coming back home after a trip and there's the laundry, unpacking, and grocery shopping to do, your cheerleader will say, "You've got this, you can do this, one step at a time."

If you're running late and starting to feel stressed, your cheerleader will say, "Take a deep breath, don't rush, all is well."

If you look at yourself in the mirror and don't like what you see, your cheerleader will say, "If you could see what I see, you are shining from the inside out, you are amazing, you are incredible, I love you."

If you feel like you're not good enough or parent, sibling, friend guilt sets in, your cheerleader will say, "You ARE good enough, tomorrow is a new day, you are learning and doing a great job."

If you're giving a speech or teaching a class and you feel insecure, your cheerleader will say, "Hey! Listen up, you showed up, you are here and people need you to be authentic. You are amazing!"

You start to hear this positive feedback from YOU, your cheerleader. The positivity starts to sink into your mind and heart. You feel lighter and the heavy weights of negativity begin to release.

Once you feel you've accomplished the Pause Method,

this process needs to be implemented every day. The ego will try to gain control every once in a while to see if it can take over.

The key is to not beat yourself up if the ego lingers and wants to remain in control. Know that if you want change, bringing awareness to your negative self-talk is one method that can help.

This is a process that will forever change you in the best possible way.

STEP 3: GRATITUDE

Gratitude is the next step to help shift your mind's awareness into the Light.

Every morning when you wake up, think of three things that you are grateful for in your life. If you're not able to think of anything, go back to the basics. I am grateful for my breath. I am grateful for my nourishment. I am grateful I can see the sky today or feel the air on my skin.

We recommend doing this exercise for a minimum of three months, every single day.

When you are in a state of gratitude, your energy shifts, and your Being moves into a higher frequency.

Doors begin to open, your Light increases, and opportunities arise.

It is consistency and repetition that are necessary for this exercise. Once the three months are complete, you will embody a more regular state of gratitude. Your mind will have shifted and gratitude will become a natural part of your life.

STEP 4: BREATH

Breath is the fourth step in shifting your awareness.

Many humans have forgotten how to breathe deeply and relax their body. Begin by placing one hand on your heart and one hand on your belly. Close your eyes and take a *slow*, deep breath in through your nose. Visualize the breath moving into the belly. Feel the belly rise like a balloon and the belly softening as you breathe out slowly through the nose.

Slowly continue this deep belly breath exercise at least ten to twenty more times. You will begin to feel your gentle heartbeat and relaxation flowing throughout your body. We recommend this exercise become a part of your daily routine. Ten to twenty slow, deep belly breaths when you rise in the morning and ten to twenty slow, deep belly breaths before you go to sleep at night. After a few weeks, observe how your breath and relaxation begin to move into a fluid state and your energy looks forward to this regular part of your routine.

STEP 5: DISTRACTION

Awareness of Distraction is the fifth step in shifting your energy into a higher vibration.

There is much distraction and stimulus surrounding your planet at this time. Telephones, social media, video games, television, and radio are lower vibration frequencies that numb and tune out your sixth senses and gifts.

By eliminating distractions, you bring your awareness to the present moment.

Try turning off the radio when you are driving in your car. Notice how this stops the constant noise. Breathe slow, mindful breaths and watch how this can help you focus on the road ahead, without the millions of thoughts inundating your mind. Focus on your deep, belly breathing when you're stopped at a light and see how this simple exercise brings your awareness to the present moment.

By eliminating distraction, your senses will heighten and you become more tuned in to the natural sounds which surround you.

You take notice of the sky and cloud formations, the flowers budding and blooming, the trees swaying in the wind, and the birds flying in the sky. There is a sense of calm when you bring your awareness to the distractions and eliminate them. You become more aware of your energy and all the signs and signals that the universe is sending you.

Another form of distraction is video games and television.

Video games are death to the mind. It has the lowest vibrational frequency that is meant to capture your mind by imprisoning your brain. There is currently an addiction around the globe to video games.

If you want to change, lock up those devices and forget about them. Particularly for boys and men, as these games invoke anger, rage, and laziness that does not serve a purpose in the ascension process and growth of one's Soul.

Physical activity is the best way to combat this addiction. For the male race and part of the female race, when anger arises, move into increased physical exertion. Biking, running, rowing, martial arts, and swimming are positive for the body and mind to release pent-up emotions.

Television has some beneficial documentaries and shows to help humanity, however, those are currently few and far between. Similar to video games, television is also an addiction. How many shows do you watch in a week? Do you feel better and full of Light and joy afterward? Is this part of your routine after work and dinner to sit down and watch your shows to "relax" and tune out?

There are lower frequencies that send negative signals to humanity through the news, commercials, and other programs on the television. We recommend creating a list of all the shows you are currently watching. Over the next month, cut that list down to half. In the second month, cut that list down to a few. In the third month, move down to one show and evaluate how you feel.

Television will eventually be a thing from the past and will be long forgotten.

Telephones and social media have also taken over the planet at this time. We advise placing the crystal Shungite over the phone to eliminate the harmful EMF rays from entering the physical body. Bring the amount of time you are spending on your phone and social media to the forefront. Begin to set up boundaries on answering your phone immediately when you get an email, text, or phone call. Unless it is an emergency, let others know you will check your phone when it's right for you. There will be a release of pressure once you have placed these boundaries and made others aware of how you will respond electronically in the future.

STEP 6: SOUL EDUCATION

Education is the sixth step to awareness. *Education of the Soul.*

We are talking about using your intuition (and yes, everyone has intuition) and finding out what naturally piques your interest. This can be a very fun and exciting step! We recommend beginning this step now and continuing this step until you leave your physical vessel.

Venture into a bookstore. What books, titles and colors are you drawn to? Go into a market and see if you like a certain table with art, food, plants, essential oils, or crystals. Were you searching the internet and saw a course come up that you were intrigued by? Were you drawn to someone's energy and felt they could help you?

This step is bringing your awareness to unlocking and tuning into your intuitive gifts. Feeling inside of you as to what feels right within your gut and NOT questioning it. Trusting yourself.

Every Soul born into this realm has a Team of Light helping them. This Team of Light are your Angels, Guides, Light Beings, and Star Seed families.

Your Team of Light along with your Higher Self can help guide you to the book, course, other materials, and people that can help you on your journey. Trust this process within your Team and your energetic fields.

STEP 7: MEDITATION

Meditation is the seventh step to awareness.

Meditation is the pausing of the mind, bringing you into the present moment. Your body requires this respite daily to function properly. As with step 6, we also recommend starting step 7 at present and continuing until you depart your physical vessel.

Here is a list of some meditation practices that we recommend. You can begin by trying each one of these practices and seeing which one works best for you. At first, it can be overwhelming and daunting with the many thoughts going through the mind. Do not give up.

Remember, meditation is a practice.

Be patient and kind with yourself when you first begin and trust that with time and commitment, *it will happen*.

Counted Breath Meditation: Begin to settle into the body by sitting on the floor or a chair. Closing your eyes, begin with three slow, deep belly breaths. In through the nose and out through the nose. Now, count to four as you breathe in, pause for a count of four, and breathe out for a count of four to six and pause. Continue this counted breath for ten more rounds. Quieting of the mind occurs when using counted breath meditation. Start in the mornings with this meditation exercise and, in a few weeks or months, add this practice before going to sleep in the evening. We recommend this practice be added to your daily routine.

Guided Meditation: There are many wonderful guided meditations you can follow online that will help you relax. The purpose of guided meditation is to shift your complete awareness to the person's voice that is speaking. We would like you to find a guided meditation that you resonate with the voice and where you can stay awake. Begin the guided meditation by waking up earlier than usual and listening to it for five to ten minutes before starting your day. This practice will begin your day with a fresh, healthy mindset.

Mantra Meditation: A Mantra is a powerful set of words or sounds. Certain sounds in the universe will shift the cells in your body and increase the Light in your Being.

When focusing and bringing your attention to the mantra, this will help still the mind.

What do you currently want to feel at this moment? Do you desire peace, calm, or joy? We recommend thinking about these questions and when you come to your answer for the day, that will be your mantra. You will begin your Mantra Meditation by sitting on the floor or a chair, your spine is tall and straight. Begin with a few deep belly breaths, in and out through the nose. Take another inhale and, as you exhale, say your mantra in your mind. With each exhale, you will repeat your mantra. It does not matter to count the number of times you are saying the mantra in the beginning. We want you to feel your breath enter the body and feel the mantra sink into your cells as you exhale.

Here are some recommended examples of Mantras for Meditation:

<u>Om</u> - (*pronounced ohm*). Om is the sound that was made when this universe was made and it is the sound that currently vibrates through the Earth at this time. This sound will clear the Soul and energy of the body consistently.

<u>Ah</u> - (*pronounced ah*). Ah is the sound that brings joy into one's one Being. People often use the sound "ah" after drinking or eating something they like. The "ah" sound in meditation vibrates through the body and raises your vibration.

<u>Hah</u> - (*pronounced hah*). Hah is the sound that will constrict the back of the throat muscles, creating a sound like the ocean, bringing relaxation into the body, mind, and Soul. When you begin this sound in your meditation, your shoulders will drop and you will feel the tension melt away from the body.

<u>Ki</u> - (*pronounced key*). Ki is the sound that opens up your awareness beyond the confines of the body. This

sound is recommended to speak softly with your hands resting in your lap and your palms facing up towards the sky. You may feel ringing in the ears and an expansion in the crown and third eye chakras. Know that all is well and you will know intuitively when this sound meditation is needed for you.

You will notice your thoughts becoming more present in the Now, as you gift your mind the continual practice of meditation and a sense of calm in your body.

STEP 8: WHAT GOES IN THE BODY?

What you put in your physical body is the eighth step we would like to bring your awareness to. *The physical vessel that you are currently in is your temple.* What you put in your body affects the physical body and can be transformational to your health.

1. Fuelling your body with organic vegetables, fruits, nuts, and seeds will help transition your Being into great health. Your body is in constant communication with you every day. The previous steps will help you to hear and understand what your body is saying to you.

2. Drinking filtered water and eliminating alcohol and caffeine will increase your communication with your body and jump-start your path to health and longevity.

Your Divine Essence resides in your physical vessel and your physical vessel works like a highly advanced computer. Your body is constantly working for you by pumping your heart and blood, eliminating what isn't needed, sending signals to the brain, and using the spine as a highway of communication.

When you fuel your body with healthy organic living greens, vegetables, and fruits, your body starts to sing on the inside and works harmoniously. You feel lighter, happier and your mind will be clear.

There are incredible advancements on your planet with clean eating. As the vibration continues to rise, much of humanity will be eating less dense food and become acutely aware of the quality of food they will be ingesting.

STEP 9: WHAT GOES ON THE BODY?

What you put *on* your body can be detrimental to your health. Bringing your awareness to what you put on your body is the ninth step to mindful awareness.

1. Begin by bringing your awareness to what you put on your body from the moment you wake up, to the moment you go to sleep. Create a list and take inventory. Some examples might be soap, shampoo, shaving cream, toothpaste, cream, deodorant, hair styling products, makeup, perfume, nail polish, clothing, hair dye, etc.

2. Some ingredients can cause cancer and other serious illnesses to the body which are found in products that you may be putting on the body. Begin to research your list one product at a time. What is in the products that go on your body? If the ingredients are not listed, do not buy that product. Find out what the ingredients are and what they mean. It may feel overwhelming at first, however, it will not take long. With your research, you will see what is currently available on the planet to cause harm to humans and the many simplistic, natural products that can both sustain and benefit the body.

3. Extend your research with what products your body is in contact with. Laundry detergents, cleaning products, sanitizers, paints, crafting materials, etc. You are now providing your awareness to expand and fall away from the illusion. You are bringing your power back to you with your own decisions and your health.

Also, do not be fooled with product labeling or with what the government has deemed as safe. Many products are labeled healthy and natural which is not the case. We advise you to always look at the ingredient list with anything that is in contact with the body.

Some products are natural, healthy, and have beneficial ingredients for the body. When you begin this journey of ingredient awareness, you will be astounded at what is created and what is available to all.

There will be a shift of awareness in humanity, as each Soul awakens to taking responsibility for what they put in and on their bodies and move into a less-is-more perspective.

STEP 10: POSTURE

Posture is the tenth step that will help you move forward at this time.

In a standing position, imagine a string at the top of your head, lift out of your waist with a straight spine, shrug your shoulders up to your ears and roll your shoulders behind you. Opening your heart through the chest, tucking the chin slightly, and placing your hands by your side. This is the posture we would like to draw to your attention.

Many humans are sitting on their computers and phones, beginning to have unnatural curvatures to the neck and spine that will cause long-term damage.

Upon waking in the morning, we recommend standing with your feet hip-distance apart on the ground, inhaling your hands high above the head, looking up at your hands, and moving into a forward fold slowly over the legs, pausing, breathing, and slowly rolling up to standing, repeating this motion several times. This gentle motion in the morning wakes up the spine and nerves in the body, slowly, before you start your day.

Check in with your body's posture throughout your day. Be aware of both feet on the Earth, your weight evenly distributed with a long spine and shoulders rolled back and a gentle tuck of the chin toward the chest. This posture will serve your body well with strong communication for the spinal network and brain.

Patience and kindness are a must with following these ten steps. If you fall back into your old ways, don't give up, try again. These steps will ground into your life when you realize how good your body and mind feel.

PART 2

LOVING ONESELF

There are 5 steps to Part 2 of this book.

Each step is peeling back the layers of the energetic fields, emotions, and conditions that have been placed on the human spirit. Take your time to read and integrate the steps, allowing your heart to lead the way.

STEP 1: FINDING OUT HOW TO LOVE ONESELF

How does one love oneself? This is a step-by-step exercise on finding out how to love yourself.

To love oneself, first bring your awareness to who you love first. Is it your parents, children, siblings, relatives, coworkers, friends, pets, animals, nature?

1. Create a list of everyone and everything you love.

2. With that list, write down next to each name, how you show your love to them. Is it by cooking for them, listening, showing up when you're needed, spending time together, showing expressions of love with hugs, kind words, and affection?

3. Next, create a list of ways you give back to yourself. This list is not focusing on buying material items for yourself. Instead, it is more focused on the acts of self-care. Do you enjoy walking in nature, having alone time, creating art or music, reading a book, or taking a bath? Do you love participating in something that brings your heart joy?

4. Take a look at the list of how you express love for your loved ones and the list of how you love yourself. Taking a look at these lists is bringing awareness to yourself. Are you truly loving yourself?

The list for loving *you* needs to be doubled as humanity

moves through ascension on this planet. If your list is currently empty on ways to love yourself, your list needs to be tripled.

To love oneself, it is important to love yourself first, without having the expectations of someone else having to do that for you. Fall in love with you.

This knowing is stepping back into your own power.

Getting into the habit of knowing when you need your alone time, and when you need to be around others, is giving back to you and loving yourself. When a Soul does this, you fill up your own heart with the awareness that this is not selfish. When loving oneself, take the time to fill up your cup. This is when you shine and can then help others at full capacity.

STEP 2: SELF-CARE

Self-care for the Soul is the second step to loving oneself.

In Part 1, there were self-care steps to help the body and mind. This step in Part 2 moves deeper into self-care of the Soul.

Stillness is <u>the</u> key to Soul care. Stillness is opening the line of communication for your human self to receive messages from your Soul. Many people are running from activities, work, and functions, that leaves the Soul spinning, ungrounded, and detached from awareness. Every day, even for a few moments, allow yourself to sit in stillness. Feel your heart beating, listen to the sounds around you and let it fade away as you breathe naturally. Bringing stillness every day into your life will bring peace to your Soul.

Be in nature and around plants and animals. Your Soul needs to be in nature. It craves it. The trees, earth, water, and sky are all elements that are essential for Soul growth. Plan your weekends including time away to be in the natural world.

If it's available to you, plant a garden in your yard, place plants in and around your home, on your deck or balcony. Plants in the home environment help to clean the air, as they are living Beings. Talk to them, sing to them, tell them you love them, care for them by watering and dusting them when needed. Watch their growth and show them your gratitude.

Spending time around animals is nurturing for your Soul. Adopt a pet if you can or spend time around people in your life who have animals of their own. Animals give humans unconditional love. They are wonderful companions and protectors to humankind. When you are with an animal, you are in the present moment and this brings the Soul pure joy.

Grounding is necessary for the Soul as the frequencies move into higher vibrations on Mother Earth. Grounding is connecting your bare feet with the earth, walking on the earth or through the water. Another option is to visualize tree roots, from your tailbone moving down your legs, through your feet, through the layers of the earth to Mother Earth's crystalline core. Connecting your roots around her core and receiving Mother Earth's anchoring energy back up through your roots into the body. Continuing to breathe as you release what you need to let go of through your roots and allow the grounding, stabilizing energy to come back into you. This exercise is beneficial to perform every day, especially when you feel energetically off from the sun activity and astrological placements.

Connection and sharing with others is the glue that binds us all together. When humans connect with other people, you feel you are not alone on your journey. The more humans share with an open heart, the quicker the process will be with releasing the lower frequencies from the body. Be vulnerable, dare to share, as the world is changing and the need for connection is stronger than ever.

STEP 3: RELEASING FEARS AND EMOTIONS

Releasing Fears and Emotions is the third step to loving

oneself. Before you enter your human body you are Divine Light consciousness. You are Light and energy. You are eternal.

This knowledge can shift one's fear of dying and fears in general. Know that when you die, you are transitioning into your purest state of energy, which is your Divine Essence.

Following through with the previous two steps will make this step easier. As soon as you decided to come to Earth, there were emotions and fear that were attached to the Soul. This is from your past lives, ancestors, and the people that conceived you. In this particular life that you are currently in, one of your life experiences is to release those emotional attachments. To do that, we move into the next step, facing our fears and releasing emotions.

Releasing Fears

Write down the fears which you carry.

Some examples may be: being alone, being abandoned, not being loved, fear of flying, fear of snakes, small spaces, heights, fire, drowning, dying.

Now we ask that you find a space in your home where you will not be disturbed and you can have access to your written fears.

Lying down, invite your Highest Self and your Team

of Light (your Guides and Light Beings) to help you release one fear at a time. Take a few long breaths into the belly and ask your Team and Highest Self for guidance. Think of your fear and with a STRONG, clear voice say three times out loud "I __say your name__ release all attachments to my fear of __state your fear__."

Say out loud three times "I now surround myself with Love and Golden Light. All attachments of my fear of __state your fear__ are released."

Say out loud once, "So be it and so it is. It is done. Thank you, thank you, thank you."

This can be an emotional experience and you may feel a weight being removed from the body and lightness in your Soul. We recommend taking your time with each fear. Breathing, asking your Team of Light and Higher Self for assistance. The conviction in your voice must be felt for this to work energetically.

Acknowledging your fears is the first step in this releasing process. Further in the chapters, we take a deeper look at fear and how it is currently surrounding humans with what is projected into society.

Releasing Emotions

How do you feel about yourself? Have you ever given yourself the time to sit down, feel and think about how you feel about yourself? This exercise is meant to bring awareness and show you how you truly feel about you. This is an important step as it brings your attention to emotions that may be buried deeply in your energetic fields. The acknowledgment of yourself will help you know what to let go of and release.

Circle the Emotions below that you currently feel for yourself:

Line 1: Love • Self-Respect • Honor • Kindness • Compassion • Empathy • Forgiveness

Line 2: Self-hatred • Self-loathing • Judgment • Jealousy • Anger • Disrespect • Shame • Guilt

These two lines shine a light on your emotions towards yourself. You can be in both lines, or fully in line 1 or line 2.

There is no right or wrong way to respond.

The ultimate goal is to be fully in line 1 in the years to come. When this is achieved, there is a deep sense of freedom for you and your Soul to shine at full capacity.

If you circled emotions from the second line, know that these emotions can change and fluctuate as you continue to work on yourself. As you move into the 5th dimension, your Soul will no longer harbor these emotions. It is through your hard work and dedication that you will move through releasing the emotions that no longer serve you.

Through time, love, and patience with oneself, being completely in the first line can happen.

Now that awareness has been brought to light with how you feel about yourself, it is time to release the emotions through memories.

1. Early Memories

Going back and remembering past traumas and memories where you felt anger, self-loathing, guilt and shame is the first step in releasing emotions. This step is a process of deep transformation for the Soul and brings freedom and release.

Take time to be with yourself and think back to your earliest memory that brought up emotions that are affecting you today. Trust in yourself that you can now deal with the memory that will surface. All of the memories will not come flooding in to overwhelm you.

This is a step-by-step process and being patient with oneself is important.

As the memory surfaces, were you a little boy or girl? Teenager or adult? What was happening around you? What happened that brought these emotions forward?

As your memory unfolds, sit with this memory of yourself. Imagine your younger self who experienced the suffering and embrace them with who you are now. Tell them what you needed to hear in the past.

Allow the emotions to move through you. Tears may flow and anger may arise. Whatever emotions appear, experience them and allow them to flow through you.

You are healing each experience by loving yourself.

Trust the process that the memory and experience will come forward when you're ready to face and release them. You do not have to relive the memory either, as you can ask your Higher Self to show you only what is needed from the memory to help you to release the emotions.

For some Souls, this can take months to years to heal and can continue until you transition into the next realm. The key is to not put a time limit on releasing the emotion. Trust in yourself and the timing in which the memory, emotion, or experience will come forward to be released.

Each memory that surfaces to be released will bring freedom and peace into the Soul. You will notice a difference in each emotion you release and the power that comes back to you.

2. *Mindful Statements* is the second step to releasing emotions and remembering who you truly are: Love.

We recommend reading the following mindful statements below and choosing one or two. Three times a day, say each statement that you chose three times out loud. When you feel you are ready and can move on from your mindful statement, choose another one and continue with this process until you feel in your heart this is no longer needed.

Over time, these mindful statements sink into the mind, body, and Soul, naturally releasing the emotions that you no longer need to carry.

I love myself completely and wholly.

I am beautiful inside and out.

I am grateful for the opportunities that are given to me.

I am good enough.

I am smart, I have talent, I am unique, I am powerful.

I like myself.

I love myself.

I forgive myself.

I shine my Light.

I am whole, complete, and loved.

My voice is strong, clear, and powerful.

Every single Soul on this planet has come to heal, forgive and to grow from experiences on some level.

3. Awareness of Emotions

Every Soul is going through an experience whether you believe it or not. They can be rich, poor, old, young, any gender, or genderless. What you see in the news, the internet, and on social media is not always what the person is going through on the inside.

Judgment, shame, and jealousy towards oneself and others are emotions that need to be released for continued growth and expansion of the Soul. When you bring awareness of these emotions to yourself, this is considered a breakthrough for the Soul. How does one know what these emotions truly are?

Here are a few examples of shame, jealousy, and judgment that you may have experienced.

When you see a person going on vacation, this may bring up feelings of jealousy and the desire to want to go on a trip as well.

Seeing a couple holding hands or kissing may bring up insecurities in yourself and your relationships. Jealousy may arise to have or want what you are observing.

Seeing a woman pregnant may bring up issues you might feel with trying to conceive a child. Emotions may rise such as shame, anger, and grief within your own body.

Seeing someone eating or having a drink might bring up body shame for you and the relationship you have with food.

Watching someone buy something or having an item that you want may bring up the feeling of jealousy or inadequacy.

Judging a person on the color of their skin, race, gender, nationality, how they speak, what they wear, where they live, and how they behave may bring up anger and resentment in yourself or deep shame and guilt.

These are a few examples of how it is to experience being a human.

Every human goes through feelings of judgment, shame, and jealousy at some point in their life.

To move through these specific feelings:

- First, there needs to be acknowledgment and awareness of what you are feeling.

• Replace that feeling with not knowing, that you do not know what that person is going through, you do not know what it is like to be in their body and you do not know their circumstances or life story.

• Send the person Love. This will rapidly shift the energy in and around you into a higher frequency.

The more often you can shift the energy when you experience feelings of judgment, shame, or guilt, the quicker the release will be of these particular emotions and more Light will enter the Soul.

STEP 4: FORGIVENESS

One of the greatest gifts you can give yourself as you move forward on your healing journey is forgiveness. To truly forgive yourself and the people that hurt you.

Here is a step-by-step process to help release forgiveness for yourself and those that hurt you.

Forgiving Oneself

• Write a letter to yourself. This letter encompasses all of the shortcomings that you may feel inside. The wrongdoings, the hurt you may have caused others and yourself. Write down what still hurts in your heart, whether it's the failed relationships, marriage, jobs, broken friendships, the hurt that may have been afflicted on your children, parents, siblings, and animals. You will know intuitively what you want to write in this letter to yourself.

• Trust that writing this letter can take time and eventually, emotions will be released. We recommend dedicating as much time as you need to this activity, as you sit with your heart, allowing it to be heard and the feelings to be released.

• When you have finished the letter, grab a can or bucket and find a safe space to burn this letter.

• Say out loud before burning your letter, "I forgive you, (state your name)." Repeat this two more times.

• Take a few slow, deep breaths and burn the letter. As the letter burns, feel the weight of these feelings move off of you. When the letter is finished burning, release the ashes onto the earth.

• After this experience, it is time for self-care. Having a bath, going to bed early and resting can help your mind and energy. Allow your Soul to fully incorporate this letting go that has taken place, for you have given the time for your heart to be heard and now the healing can begin.

Forgiving Others

Write a letter to the person(s) that you continue to think of who may have hurt you in the past. Perhaps they affected your job, school, relationships, etc. You will know in your heart to whom you are meant to write a letter. Write everything out in this letter, what they did to you, how it has affected you, and anything else that you wish to release. Feelings of anger, fear, and sorrow may be some of the emotions you will experience as you craft your letter. Take the time to let the feelings pour out of you. Write everything that you want to say and write it without abandonment.

• Once you've finished the letter, get a bucket or can that you can burn the letter in and find a safe space where you can do so.

• Say three times out loud before you light it, "I release all emotions that no longer serve me from 'state the person's name'."

• Light the letter using a match or lighter. Now say out loud, "I forgive 'person's name'. I forgive 'person's name'. I forgive 'person's name'. This is now removed from my Being, Soul, and every part of me. So be it and so it is."

• Watch the emotions release and the letter burn, disintegrating into the cosmos. Breathe slowly. Release the ashes onto the earth.

You did it! This can be a powerful experience, so ensure you take the time afterward to take care of yourself. Know that because you have forgiven this person does not mean they will necessarily be in your life again. This is a forgiveness exercise for the Soul to release and bring freedom and movement into one's life.

When you think of this person again, take note of how you feel in your body. When you feel differently about them, and no longer feel triggered or reactive, that is when you know you have forgiven them and are ready to move on.

This exercise communicates with your energetic fields that you do not want to hold onto the shackles of thinking about this person anymore and releases what no longer serves you.

STEP 5: MOVEMENT

Movement is the fifth step in loving oneself. This part of your awareness will help your mind, body and Soul.

Daily movement is essential to the body that you are in. The body needs to be exercised every day. We recommend gentle movements such as walking, yoga, mindful dance, biking, swimming, hiking, and stretching.

There is less illness and injury to the body with gentle movement. Getting fresh air and observing your surroundings while you exercise is also beneficial to the body. These steps are all connected. As you walk, you can take notice of the beautiful trees in front of you and give gratitude to the trees that provide oxygen to the planet. You breathe deeply as you walk, feeling the air move into the body, bringing you a sense of peace. Your thoughts have moved into stillness as you practice daily meditation, bringing you into the present moment. Love for oneself surrounds your Being and the planet as you feel the sun on your skin.

All of these chapters in the book so far are here to help awaken the Soul and prepare you for the next phase of evolution on the planet.

EARTH'S STORY

We would like to continue with the story of Earth and how you all came to be at this moment in time. As worlds and species were born so too was awareness.

Even though each human originated from Source, one can fall or be coerced into a different way of being.

Throughout billions of years, Galactic wars have been going on, and to this day, wars are still happening.

These Galactic wars are fighting for control and power over planets, species and encouraging division.

Many people are drawn to science fiction movies and

television shows because all Souls on Earth have been a different species other than human and all have lived on different planets at some point.

We all originate from Source as One, however, this can be forgotten in other realms and creations throughout the different realities.

Planet Earth is a newer planet that was created from the 5th dimension planet Terra.

There have been many stories created on Earth about Earth being a Soul school and the Lightworkers coming to assist the planet and humanity from the depths of this illusion.

In part, some of this is true, as the many Lightworkers that are here now have come forth to help aid in humanity's ascension. However, many are also here to heal their karma and trauma around their past lives on Earth, which happened many thousands of years ago.

The Lightworkers that are here now are teachers and holders of the Light to help shift the illusion on Earth as you move into a higher frequency. The Lightworkers, Star Seeds, and all Souls on Earth are here to heal and forgive themselves from past experiences in their current and past lives.

Even within this illusion, there is a reality that exists and feels real to all that live here on Earth.

Within this higher frequency that is now emerging, the forces that created this entrapment will be in charge no longer. Humanity is awakening from the slumber they have been in.

The forces at hand have created a world of disconnection from your true self, your heart, using fear, chaos, and illusion. They have created a world of false pleasure with distractions, numbing the senses and the mind.

They have created disharmony in the food system and have begun poisoning the planet so the animals and eventually the humans would die off so they could have this planet all for themselves.

Why is there such an imbalance between the rich and poor? Why is there corruption in politics, the media, and worldly affairs? These forces which have taken charge are in human form and cause deliberate disruption.

Now is the time that many Souls have been waiting for: a time of higher frequency. The tides are changing and Earth and the Souls on this planet are in the Great Awakening.

As the energy continues to rise, each Soul will move into its own awakening. This is not an easy task, as you will quickly go through the layers of releasing, clearing, and healing at an accelerated rate.

LIGHTWORKERS

Currently, there are several million Lightworkers on the planet. Many are here to hold the Light for humanity and Mother Earth. Other Lightworkers are here to implement change and advancement in technology to create balance once again on this planet.

Lightworkers have taken a great responsibility to hold space and Light for Mother Earth. Energies and emotions move through the Lightworkers as they transform them into Light. Solitude is essential at certain times for Lightworkers as they hold and maintain the higher Light frequency.

You are a Lightworker if you feel you are here to help Earth and humanity on some level.

When you come across a Lightworker, you will likely be drawn to them. They can instantly put you at ease with their presence. Some Lightworkers will glow as we move forward in time. Lightworkers also need space to recharge and there will be the understanding of respecting this solitude for all Souls. Know that no Soul is above anyone else, and not to put Lightworkers or any other Beings on a pedestal. For we all come from one Source of energy and it is your heart that will be your guiding force.

As the light anchors...

Over the next 10 years, the ones that continue with greed and coercion will lose their grip on humanity and the planet.

As each of your gifts awaken, you will *feel* who is true to the Light within your Heart and Soul.

Respect, Honor, and Love are what are coming forward in the years to come. Those that do not follow with their heart, will be lost, confused, and emotionally withdrawn. There is a choice that each Soul has made before incarnating here to move into the 5th dimension or to continue to learn in the 3rd dimension. There is no right or wrong decision either way.

In the 5th dimension, *Love is the key to all.* As the energy continues to rise, when arguing with someone, ask yourself how would Love respond? In all things, ask how would Love respond? Your answer is shifted to compassion and a higher power. The ego diminishes and you feel within your heart what is true for you.

CHANGES TO COME...

Did you know that trees and whales are the wisdom keepers of Earth?

Each planet, holographic or not, holds ancient

records with an energetic grid for existence and an energetic signature. The trees hold ancient knowledge of Terra and beyond. Why is it that you feel so good when walking in a forest?

The trees, fauna, and air in a forest clear your energetic fields and fill you with grounding energy. All trees are unique and sacred. When cutting down a tree, there is a ceremony that can be done to thank the tree for its life, wisdom, and knowledge. Surround the tree with your love and ask the frequencies of the Earth to remove the life force of the tree and transmute its energy back into the cosmos.

The whales hold sacred knowledge about your Earth and ancient civilizations. All whaling must come to an end, as it is one of humanity's greatest downfalls hunting these sacred ancestors of the ocean. Whales being held in captivity will end, as there will only be ocean rehabilitation centers in the years to come.

Zoos will be a thing from the past, as all animals will be held in the utmost esteem of respect and Love. Animals communicate and have a language that all humans can partake in through observation from afar.

Hunting for sport will soon come to an end as humanity rises in ascension. There will be species that come back to the planet as people shift their awareness. Elementals, fairies, unicorns, and dragons will be once more.

These incredible Beings will appear as the energy shifts. It will not magically happen overnight, however, it will be at a much more rapid pace as the frequency increases.

This is not to bring in fear that all the 3D illusions will collapse at once. This will be a welcomed change, as your energy will not be the same as it is now. Each Soul continues to grow and expand as the energy rises. Again, this is at an accelerated rate and every Soul that is here now on planet Earth has chosen to be here for this grand awakening and shifting into the Light.

There are large crystals underneath the Earth's surface that will rise and lands will reappear that were long forgotten. There will be much less focus on materialism and greater awareness of one's strengths and uniqueness. There will be products available that will only be beneficial to the body, Earth, and atmosphere.

In the years to come, projects will present themselves that you will feel a need to partake in. Activism will rise within you and deep passion will set in as you stand up for your beliefs. This will happen to all who awaken. *Over 80%* of the planet *will awaken.*

You will begin to feel alive and experience more happiness than ever before, knowing that we are all connected as One. You are all Souls wanting to learn, grow, experience, and help Mother Earth ascend into the Light.

There will be teachers you will be drawn to for a period

of time to help you ascend and that will shift again as you rise in your ascension and move to another teacher.

Be aware there is no ultimate guru that will heal you instantly and shift you into enlightenment. This journey is yours and yours alone. Teachers, books, healers, and others can help you along the way, however, the path is sacred and must be yours to choose. You do not want to acquire karma while asking others to do the work for you.

Love is the way through on your journey, through your life lessons, through your trials and tribulations. You did not come to Earth because it was easy. You came to Earth because you knew you would grow, you would expand, you would learn from your experiences.

When you begin to break destructive cycles from your family, ancestors, and society, deep growth and healing begin to take place. Knowing that you are not your parents or your ancestors who came before you, brings in a knowing that you are your own person and you can choose your own path.

Every challenging situation and experience is an opportunity for growth. When you are down the deep dark hole of your experience, it may feel as though there is no Light at the end of the tunnel. Through your determination and motivation, you will always be able to break free. The Light will shine once again until your next experience to learn.

Life may seem unfair at times, especially when humans witness animals and children suffering. Know that some of these animals and children are Souls and have either asked for certain life experiences to grow from or are helping others in their Soul contracts with their life experiences. Many horrific, unimaginable events have taken place and are being brought to Light for humanity to see and shift as the frequency moves into a higher vibration.

PART 3

DEEPER AWARENESS

MANIFESTATION

Did you know you can create any reality you want? You can become anything you want to be.

As humanity and the planet ascends, the majority of humans will move into a higher frequency. Within this higher state, brings in emotions that will help cultivate the manifestation of your dreams into reality very quickly.

Being in joy, happiness, optimism, and love are feelings of pure Light. When feeling these emotions, be mindful of your powerful thoughts, for what you think will soon appear. When thinking of someone, they will call or appear in your life. When liking a stone or plant and wanting it, it will magically manifest. When you know anything is possible, all you have to do is think about it, you become aware of the great responsibility and care towards one's thoughts. Love, compassion, acceptance, and Light will be the way of the mind in the years to come.

To be in the present moment, we recommend paying attention to what is in front of you without distraction. Observe your surroundings and keep your mind clear. With this practice, your senses awaken and you are in a whole new world of freedom and enlightenment. Your mind is expansive and can do unimaginable things to the current mind. You will be able to leave the body and visit other lands and dimensions while your body sleeps and you will remember in the morning.

Embodying joy and laughter are aspects of Soul happiness that raise one's frequency. When you laugh and enjoy yourself, your Light shines bright and expands. Others will feel the joy rising in you and will want to partake in what you are feeling.

We are asking each Soul at this time to think of the bigger picture of their lives.

What do you want to be for your highest good?

Who do you want to be for your highest good?

How do you want to help others for your highest good?

Each of these three questions needs to have *for my highest good* after each question mark. These four words *for my highest good* take your wants and desires to the next level.

These are Soul searching questions that take time and contemplation. When answering these questions throughout your life, you may have different answers as you continue to grow and release the layers.

In many cases, you won't quite understand who you are, what you want to do, or how you want to help others. Ask your Multidimensional Highest Self to help guide you if you need assistance.

The previous parts in the book will help clear the mind, body, and Soul for you to answer the three questions above in a more focused way. Trust that you will know the answers in time if you do not know them now.

SIMPLIFY

Simplifying one's life will attract more room for happiness and joy. Here are some simple tools and questions that can bring more simplicity into your life, which creates more space for the mind to become clear.

Home

Decluttering your home and closet will bring in a flow of energy into one's space and mind. We recommend going through one's home from top to bottom, with the mindset that you are moving into a much smaller space. Sell, discard and donate items that you no longer need. This process takes time and can be a very cleansing activity to do for one's home, energy, and Soul.

Relationships

Taking inventory of your relationships is the next step to simplifying one's life.

Friends: You don't need a lot of friends to be happy and

joy-filled. Simplify your friendships by asking yourself:

Does this person love me completely and unconditionally for who I am?

Does this person have my back?

Do I feel good when I am around this person or does this person deplete me?

Can I completely be myself around this person with no judgment?

These questions will help simplify your relationships to release, maintain or add a few key people in your life that will help you grow and expand. Once this process is complete you will have friends you will truly enjoy being around.

Family: Family can be a different matter. You chose your parents and family when you entered this planet on an energetic level. This does not mean they need to be in your loving circle of relationships if there has been pain, trauma, or discord. Family can be complicated but know you have chosen your family at birth to help you experience and grow. That may mean that you love your family from afar if boundaries have been crossed. Love is the key here. Once you have forgiven family members who have hurt you, you can love them and send love to them from afar if this speaks to you. Healing will be a much quicker process once forgiveness and Love are attained.

Commitment

Commitment is the next step to simplifying your life. Commitment in relationships, work and life.

Commitment in relationships: Commitment within a relationship is more than staying with your partner in good times and bad.

It is about facing yourself and your thoughts. Look at how you feel about the relationship and what comes up for you.

To help you, ask yourself these three questions:

Does your partner respect and support you (mentally, emotionally, physically, and spiritually), the way that you need them to?

Are you in love with your partner?

Do you want to continue being with your partner?

Now ask these three questions to your partner, if possible:

Does your partner feel that you respect and support them to meet their needs?

Are they in love with you?

Do they want to continue being with you?

If answering yes to all of these questions, you are both in agreement that your relationship is united. If answering no to any of these questions, it is time to take a deeper look at why you are in this relationship.

Sit with each question and trust in your heart that when you dive into your answers, you will know what to do moving forward.

Some emotions will come up when you take a deep look at the relationship that you are in.

Fear and *Guilt* may come up if you've fallen out of love with your partner, no longer having respect for them and not trusting them or yourself.

Regret and *Anger* may be felt when looking at the relationship, with yourself and your partner.

Loss and *Grief* may also arise as a new path is formed with leaving the relationship or moving forward.

Trust that you, yourself, have the answers.

When loving yourself completely, what needs to change and happen for ALL of the questions above to be a yes? Write down what comes up in your heart. Sit with this and trust once again that as you address the situation with your heart, you will know how to proceed.

Your path to ascension is to Love oneself completely.

If your partner has cheated on you, what needs to be released to move on and forgive? It may be that you leave the relationship and your commitment to oneself becomes an unbreakable bond to love oneself.

It may be that you don't want to leave your partner after they've been unfaithful. You're willing to work together to strengthen your relationship with communication and trust.

This may also be a lesson or experience in facing your fears and gaining the courage to leave the relationship when you know in your gut, in your heart, it is the best thing for you, your partner, and your family.

Couples often stay together to keep the family bonded, thinking this is the best solution for the children. This process will no longer work in the energy that humanity is moving into.

Children are highly sensitive beings and feel the emotions and energy that radiate off of both parents in their home(s).

When needing to separate yourself from the relationship, give gratitude and love to your partner for the lessons that were learned. If children were part of the relationship, send love and gratitude to your partner for the creation of the beautiful being(s) that you created or raised together. Send love to your partner and that is it. Keep it simple. For this is a part of their journey and path to take on their own now, even if it is still intertwined with the children. Be mindful of the negative emotions that can eat away at one's Soul if one continues to harbor ill feelings towards one's past or current partner. Forgiveness is the key. Seek counsel and support to help move the emotions once one has sat and felt them fully.

Your children will feel the flowing energy in your home once you've taken the courage to Love oneself completely and let go of what no longer serves you. Your children will grow from your experience and learn to have respect, honor, and Love for one another and themselves as they watch and observe what true love looks like for oneself. That in itself is truly a gift to give back to both yourself and your children.

Couples can also stay together for financial reasons. On Earth, it can be costly to separate or divorce your partner. No matter the reason for staying together, if you are not happy in your partnership, you will feel this deeper and deeper in the coming years ahead. The issues will need to be addressed as they will become unbearable in the heart, as the energies increase.

It takes deep courage to move forward out of the relationship that is no longer serving you. Whatever the circumstances might be, trust in your heart you will be ready to take the next step when it is time.

If leaving the relationship, proceed with a cord-cutting ceremony. This can be done by yourself, in the privacy of your own home.

Close your eyes, visualize yourself and your partner directly across from you, and an energetic cord connecting you both between your navels. Take a few long, deep, belly breaths. Imagine a golden pair of scissors coming to the middle of the cord that connects you. On the count of three, in the next few moments, the scissors will cut the cord. First, take a slow deep breath in, pause and as you breathe out, say out loud:

"All energy that is mine comes back to me now and all energy that is my partners goes back to them now. One, two, three." Visualize the cord being cut with the golden scissors.

Bow deeply to your partner, thanking them for the time and experiences you had together. Take in another few deep breaths and slowly open your eyes. Take a moment to sit with your emotions and reflect on how you feel.

Commitment in work: Commitment in your work is giving it your all and not giving up. It's more than just showing up and doing the basic job at hand. It's about going above and beyond, putting your heart, energy, and Soul into the work. Following this commitment pays off as it will lead you to where you are meant to be.

Not knowing what you want to do for a career path is completely acceptable. There is too much pressure after high school, as you grow and age that you should know exactly what you want to do.

Releasing that idea and moving forward with the intention, you are exactly where you need to be, will help.

Yes, some Souls know their calling early on in life. That is not to say they are more advanced than others, their path is just different. Honor where you are and be curious about what life has to offer all around you. See what piques your interest, take courses, read books, travel. Eventually, your path will seem less daunting and it will align with your interests and desires.

Our channeler Sarah went along her journey finding out what worked and what didn't work for her. There were a few things that interested her and she started to follow that path, however, she did not know she would be doing this type of work years later. Through curiosity and committing fully to the job that she had at the moment, she arrived at her destiny while trusting herself and her path.

Whether you're working at a gas station, bank, hardware store, restaurant, or any other job, give it your all, wherever you are.

If you are in a job that you don't enjoy, keep exploring and searching in your spare time. Move forward with what you feel guided to do. Trust in this process. This will not happen overnight or in the blink of an eye, but it will happen.

Commitment in life: Commitment in life is about being your authentic self. To show up and be proud of who you are. Find out who you are and take the time that is needed to do so.

What do you want out of life right now? Keep asking yourself this question once it has been answered: ask the question, how can your life get better?

Your answer will change as you grow through your experiences and shift into the higher frequencies.

FEAR, LOSS, AND TRANSITION

Fear is an emotion that cuts you off from your Light and Source. Everyone experiences fear at some point in their lives as a Soul. There are many things, places, and events that can trigger fear in oneself.

Past lives, people, trauma, sickness, age, and the unknown can cause a rise in fear that stops one's life in its tracks.

To get through the fear is to face it head-on with Light, *asking for help* from your Higher Self and your Team of Light and knowing that you are Eternal. Your Higher Self and Team of Light may guide you to a therapist, healer, teacher, course, or a book that will help unlock the fear. Once you've asked for help, be open to seeing the signs that are presented to you. Fear can also propel you forward into a strength that you never knew you had. It can shine awareness on what needs to be addressed.

Loss is not easy for those who have experienced a death in their life. It can feel that the world keeps moving around you when your world has completely stopped. You may feel your life becomes dull and gray, while your whole Being feels numb. You may not be able to eat food and find it tasteless. You may feel tired, depleted, depressed, and withdraw from life around you.

We share with you a few steps to communicate with your loved ones who have transitioned to the other side. This will help you know that there is only a doorway between the two of you, as you will meet again and there is a new way of communicating with one another.

1. Signs and Symbols

Before your loved one crosses over, talk to them about what symbol(s) they will send you to let you know they are near and they are ok. If this is not a possibility, you can ask for a sign or symbol after they have transitioned.

Here are some examples of signs and symbols from those that have crossed over: rainbows, cloud formations, birds, feathers, coins, animals, songs, and words. Be patient with seeing or hearing the sign and symbol and know it may not come in the form you expect. If you ask for a coin, it may show up in a picture or book, instead of a coin in your hand.

2. Stillness

Providing quiet for your mind and being in the present moment allows communication from the next realm to come in with your loved one's messages who have crossed over. Automatic writing can also be a form of communication. In stillness, breathe mindfully, sit with a notebook and pen, ask your loved one a question, and with patience and time, your hand will begin to write the answers. The ego will try to enter here saying this is your mind, give up, this is not you. Do not pay attention to the ego, over time your confidence will grow and you will know it is your loved one on the other side who responds.

3. Dreams

Dreams are a wonderful way to see, hear and feel your loved ones again. Know that your loved ones can not be in your dreams every night but cherish the dream(s) when they do come through. It does not matter if you do not understand the dream, what matters is that you saw, heard, or felt your loved one and they came through for you, to be able to receive that beautiful moment. Once awakening from your dream, send thanks to your loved ones as it is not always easy to communicate in this way.

Dreams are a gateway between the spiritual world and the world that you are currently in. Dreams can release what you need to let go of and welcome important messages. There are currently other dimensions and timelines around your life that you are in. When you experience deja vu, you are experiencing what you have seen from one of your other timelines or a moment that will happen in the future.

Transition is the step when it is time to leave your physical body and move into the Light, into your Multidimensional Highest Self.

Many people fear death as they believe it is the final end and this can bring up a deep attachment, clinging to life here on Earth.

When you leave your physical vessel, you are transitioning into the next realm of Light which is your true home of All That Is. It is a doorway from one world to the next. If you knew the deep love felt on the other side, there would not be a clinging attachment to the physical body, instead, there would be rejoicing and happiness leading the way.

When crossing over, your Team of Light, past loved ones, and your pets are awaiting your arrival. It is a very joyous time to reconnect to the Souls that have been patiently awaiting.

ENERGY CONNECTION

Once you have gone through the previous steps, you may begin to feel the connection in all living things. Humans, animals, plants, trees, rocks, minerals, crystals, and Mother Earth, we are all connected and that connection weaving us together is energy.

As humans move forward as a species, some of you will be able to see, feel, hear, sense, and even smell and taste energy. Listed below are sensory extensions of energy that can open within each one of you.

Someone who can see energy is <u>clairvoyant</u>. This can be in the form of seeing visions, other Light Beings, or the matrix around you.

Someone who can feel energy is <u>clairsentient</u>. This person can deeply feel the emotions of others, know when they are lying, feel someone else's pain in their own body or feel the energy of a room before entering.

Someone who can hear energy is <u>clairaudient</u>. This person has highly sensitive hearing, can hear other sounds before others, can hear sounds from different realms, and can hear voices from higher vibrations.

Someone who can smell energy has <u>clairalience</u>. This person can smell scents from the other realms. If there is a grandmother who has crossed over and her sign was roses, they will have the ability to smell roses and there will be no roses around them. They will have a heightened sensitivity to all scents as well.

Someone who can taste energy is <u>clairgustance</u>. This person can taste foods when those foods are not physically around, these signs can be from past loved ones letting you know they are there. This person can also have a heightened sensitivity to taste. An example would be tasting a preservative in food that no one else can taste.

Someone who knows energy is <u>claircognizant</u>. This person receives information from a higher source and feels it in the gut and heart. Information can also be channeled through this person and they can have prophetic dreams.

Every human on Earth has one or more of these abilities and beyond.

Know that dedication to yourself and finding out who you are, will help to expand your senses. Feel the connection with one another, the Earth, trees, plants, and animals, as you are all ascending together.

The more you work on yourself: letting go, healing, and forgiving, the more you will open to a oneness mentality for the higher good of ALL.

ENVIRONMENT

Your environment around you will change as the world transitions.

The Earth can no longer continue with the way humanity is treating her.

As the world goes through life-altering changes, humanity will begin to go back to the stillness of observing and watching nature and the beauty all around. Nature teaches us all how life exists. There is a beginning, an ending, and magic in between.

At this time, we would like humanity to take a look at your body environment, home environment, and work and school environment. Under each category are points for you to examine in your life to reach the maximum growth and full potential of happiness and joy.

Body Environment

What does your body need to survive? Air, water, and nourishment.

Let's take it a step further, what does your body need to survive in a balanced, mental, emotional, physical, and spiritual environment?

The following points under each category bring awareness on how your Soul will thrive in each of these categories.

Mentally

• Spend time around people who love and support you unconditionally.

• Respect and honor your personal boundaries and follow through with them.

• Release past traumas and move forward with ease.

Emotionally

• Release negative emotions and feelings.

• Forgive oneself and others and move forward.

• Allow Love and Light to enter the body and accept this wholeheartedly.

Physically

• Exercise the body every day.

• Provide clean air for your body to breathe.

• Provide healthy, nourishing foods for the body to digest.

• Drink clean, filtered water every day.

• Eliminate preservatives and processed foods from your diet.

Spiritually

• Set up a ritual of daily meditation or prayer.

• Breathe deep, slow, relaxed breaths.

• Sit in stillness daily.

Home Environment

What does your environment look like around your home? Is it cluttered and messy? Clean and organized? Here are a few steps we recommend to attain a clear, energetic space in your home.

- Take the time to declutter your home

- Clean your home thoroughly from top to bottom

- Bring in houseplants to cleanse the air

- Open all the windows, doors, closets, and drawers of every room in your house and smoke cleanse your home either with an energy clearing spray or a smoke cleansing wand. When beginning, go into the four corners of each room and say "I release all negativity and darkness from this room, only Love and Light remain." If you are burning a smoke wand, be mindful of the embers, have a shell or bowl underneath, as the debris releases ash as it burns.

- Remove all belongings and materials that do not feel good to you.

Tune in with the energy of your home after these steps are complete. Your space will feel renewed, peaceful and calm.

Work and School Environment

When you are not given a choice on who you go to school and work with, it can be challenging. We recommend the following steps to attain peace in your work and school environment.

• Protecting your energy in the morning and night can help immensely while being around others' energy. Visualize a golden bubble of Light around you and all negativity and other energies other than your own, bouncing off of your bubble. Set an intention for this to be so and that your golden bubble will protect you. Continue to place this bubble of Light around you as many times as you see fit throughout your day. Over time, you will feel the bubble of Light strengthen and you may not need to surround yourself as often as the energies increase with frequency on your planet.

• Showing compassion to each other will also help you be in a supported work/school environment. When expressing compassion, it raises your frequency and Love takes hold.

• Breathing in slow, deep breaths before an exam or when dealing with other intense energies can help calm the body instantly.

• Breathing slow, deep breaths while at work when dealing with a challenging personality will help shift the energy into a more peaceful state, bringing forward the mentality that this is not your energy.

NEW WAY OF BEING

When focusing on clearing and healing one's emotions in the heart, your frequency shifts into a higher vibration. This is where humanity is now going, into a higher vibration.

There will be less materialism and traveling in your world as deeper and more meaningful connections take hold.

The virus that is currently affecting humanity and the world will eventually subside and there will be changes that take place for the betterment of all. There needs to be a deeper look at your day-to-day job, what you are doing, where it is located, and if it is necessary.

This will be a time of eliminating many industries that take a toll on the environment. This is a necessary evolution that is needed for humanity and your planet to survive.

The new way of engaging moving forward will be based on the heart.

Some Souls that are not ready or do not want to partake in moving ahead will leave this planet through death from disease, sickness, and other ailments. The Souls that will cross over have already had the experiences they needed and we honor them for their journey. Take note, these Souls have passed through a doorway and you will see them again.

CHANGES IN THE HUMAN BODY

The human body will go through a series of changes as humanity moves ahead to the New Earth.

There will also be a shift in what humans consume in their bodies.

There will be no animal products that cause harm to any animal. Home-cooked meals and learning the ways of your ancestors through storing and canning food will be revived. This will be brought into all communities as there will be more of a communal way of living.

Water will become cleaner and more alkaline, helping the body adapt to these changes. Certain products will no longer exist as they are poisonous and cause detrimental harm to the physical body.

The body will increase in Light. The mind will become clearer and more love will come in. There will be a joyous way of life and happiness will be experienced daily.

As the body increases in Light, so too, will the mind expand. Each of you will connect daily with your guidance through your Multidimensional Highest Self and your Team of Light. This will decrease loneliness and enable people to feel more connected.

As the mind expands, creativity will increase and you will be drawn to activities that may be new to you.

Writing, art, music, dance, singing, building, and creating projects will come forward and your past lives will join with this one. In your past lives, you may have been an artist, a singer, an oracle, a herbalist, these gifts that you once had will now come forward merging with who you are now.

There are body sensations that may arise as it increases in Light. When these sensations come forward, send gratitude to the body and increase your water intake to eight to ten glasses a day to help flush out the toxins.

Here are a few examples of the body sensations that you may experience at different times of your ascension:

Body Sensations

- Aches and pains in the body

- Headaches

- Taste sensitivity

- Ear ringing

- Hearing high pitched frequencies

- Nausea

- Heart opening

• Pressure in the crown and third eye

• Jaw and teeth discomfort

• Having to clear the throat

• Hunger

• Increased thirst

• Feeling body heat rise, hot flashes

• Feeling tired, lethargy, and moments of exhaustion

• Seeing rays of colors, sparkling flashes of Light or orbs of Light

• Feeling vibrations, energy running throughout the body

• Feeling other Light Beings presences

• Feeling warmth in the chest

• Seeing golden Light around your body

Tools to help alleviate some of these sensations are:

• Saltwater baths.

• Drinking increased water as mentioned above.

• Sleep and rest when you can. This includes ten to fifteen-minute naps in the day when needed.

• Grounding into the Earth: mindfully walking barefoot on the Earth, in the ocean, or freshwater.

• Sitting or laying in the sunshine for ten minutes at a time. The sun is healing to the body and you will feel this throughout your Being.

• Laughing: laughter raises your vibration and brings ease to the aches and pains.

• Gentle movement such as yoga, stretching, or walking helps the energy to keep flowing through your body.

The body will begin to look slightly different and change shape as humans ascend.

Bodies will begin to elongate and the head shape will become a bit larger.

Posture will become incredibly straight and the chest will enlarge slightly.

There will be sustainable clothing that humanity will wear. Natural fabrics with no synthetics.

The sun will intensify as your body and eyes adjust to more Light.

This new way of life will be simple and rewarding in

the day-to-day process. Advanced technology will help humans live in a prosperous way that aligns with Mother Earth.

Travel will cease for many as the desire lessens, bringing the pollution levels to decrease.

Nature will return to the natural order and fish stocks and other animal species will replenish.

Humans will go back to the elements of the Earth to heal. Pharmaceutical companies will be a thing from the past. Plant medicines, bodywork, energy work, and expansion of the mind will be the healing that people need to move forward in optimal health.

Portals that had once been closed will open again as the frequency rises. These portals are a connection to other dimensions that will open in the next ten to fifteen years. In the present state, humanity will focus on healing oneself internally and no longer seek the quick thrills that offer no resolution or guidance.

When these portals open, access will occur to the realms that had once been closed off to protect the rest of the universe from the darkness spreading on Earth. Communication will proceed with other species in the universes. Other worlds will open up to the human race providing adventure and otherworldly possibilities of expansion. Imagine no materialism, no celebrities, no politics, no unnecessary drama, no more wasted time with artificial joy.

This is the way of the New Earth, going back to the ways of the land, simplifying one's life, honoring and respecting all living Beings.

Moving forward, there will be uncertainty in the next few years with the collective of humanity. Changes will be vast as the energy shifts at an increased rate. Many people will decide to not have children in the years to come, and many will adopt children that currently need loving homes.

If adults do want their own children, there will only be one to two births per couple. Humanity will know having large families cannot sustain the Earth as the energy rises.

Love, compassion, and gratitude will lead the way of the new world. There will be the constant mindset of helping one another, open communication, and living from your heart center.

As the body changes with the increase of Light on the planet, so too will the amount of food one individual needs to sustain itself in the physical body. Food will be eaten mindfully and the realization that the intake of healthy vegetables and fruits is only what is needed.

Long ago, other civilizations came to Earth to help create and build temples and pyramids to advance the human race.

This information will be revealed to your planet as the vibration increases. Some civilizations that were here on

Earth long ago will return to help humans advance in their technology. This time, the technology will stay and Earth will rebalance to a long-forgotten time of Eden.

HYBRIDS

There are many hybrids currently living on Earth. These hybrids have different DNA than other human beings. Their DNA is marked when they will remember or accelerate into their mission at certain moments in their lives. The mission of the hybrids is to help humanity ascend.

Some hybrids will be revealed over time. We recommend listening to what they have to offer to humanity and yourself for growth and expansion.

DISCERNMENT, CURIOSITY AND CREATIVITY

Many secrets and hidden knowledge of your planet will be revealed over the next coming years.

If humans were to know the bigger picture all at once, it would be too much for the Soul to manage. As the energy shifts and your minds begin to expand, more knowledge will come forward. When a Soul is in a heavier dimension such as the 3rd dimension, there are belief systems and controls over the population. The majority of humanity is now shifting into the 4th and 5th dimensions and that brings transition.

As a collective, we recommend always using your discernment with any energy you come in contact with and any situation or dimension that you are in.

The way of humanity moving forward is to grow as a species in love and acceptance without the controls and shackles which have plagued this planet for centuries. Mother Earth is your ally and can bring about great healing and grounding to one's Soul.

Centuries ago, when humanity began at the lowest depths of greed and corruption, the High Councils in the twelfth dimension placed the call throughout the multiverse to help planet Earth. Many Souls heard the call of help and a plan was put in motion to bring the Light to balance once again.

The High Councils knew this process would take hundreds of years to balance the tipping of the scales.

That time is now dear ones. The tipping of the scales is happening. Structures that no longer support humanity are crumbling. New structures and ways of being are unfolding behind the scenes. We ask that you have patience. Focus on gratitude and looking within oneself. Release the layers that no longer serve you, as this will help your process so much more.

Every Soul on this planet has asked to be here during this time. It is a time of great celebration as there is much to look forward to in the coming years. Growth is the expansion of the Soul. You are all growing through your experiences and there are millions of other Beings watching from afar that are in awe of what you are doing and how you are helping others.

What happens on Earth has a ripple effect in this universe and out into the cosmos. The knowledge that is learned here will help other planets, realms, and universes. There is a much bigger picture here than the life that you currently lead on your planet. We say this not to diminish the importance of your life, but to bring awareness to each one of you.

Now is the time to slow down and reevaluate your life. This place in time is a gift to you, to open your heart, forgive others, forgive yourself and discover what lights up your world. What are you passionate about?

Find the spark that speaks to your Soul which brings you joy, excitement, and curiosity.

Curiosity and creativity will lead you down the path to your Soul's purpose.

Trust that you have a Team of Guides and Light Beings surrounding you who are assisting you on your journey. You may be able to feel them with physical reactions from your body, such as goosebumps or cold air on the skin. One may feel their energy of love and acceptance in the space that you are in and others will be able to see orbs with their very own eyes and in the pictures that you take.

Yes, your Team of Light and your Guides have agreed and signed a contract to help you in this lifetime.

It is your Multidimensional Highest Self that is with you always. You are an aspect of your Highest Self. When connecting with this higher aspect of you, there is a sense of expansion in your Being, your magnificent Light and you will never forget this experience.

There are Legions of Angels that surround your planet as well. There are Angels who help the plants and vegetation and communicate with the trees and the Elementals. Some Angels are in the sky, clearing the air and bringing signs and symbols down from the clouds to you.

Once the acknowledgment is made that you have a Team of Light helping you AND you begin to ask for their help for your highest good, of one hundred percent pure Light. *This is now the game changer for you in the advancement of one's Soul with your continued inner-work.* When the acknowledgment is made when asking for help with using one hundred percent pure Light for your highest good, this statement clarifies to other Souls and entities that only the highest Light quotient is to be aiding you.

At this stage, the question arises, "Why am I here?"

You are here to grow as a Soul, to heal and forgive. You have experienced many other lifetimes as a Soul. Many have trained in their previous lives to be here now, in this specific timeline to be able to complete the karmic cycle and rise as a collective together.

In addition to healing and forgiveness, your Soul may have heard the call from the High Councils to help Mother Earth and humanity to balance the Light.

The virus is the first step of many that will help humanity get to the place of oneness with each other and the planet you currently live on. When the virus was released, the Beings that created this intended to eradicate the majority of humans. This is but one truth.

Another truth that comes forward is, this is a program, a grand design, from the higher realms to help evolve humanity. How does a virus that has killed many and impacted the entire planet, help humanity?

For many people, this was to show each one of you what matters the most: your relationship with yourself, your body, the people that uplift your spirit, and your relationship with your planet.

The virus will not affect those that do not have a lesson to learn or need a cleansing throughout their body.

This is not to say that if you received the virus you have a low vibration, and it is not to say, for the Souls that did not contract the virus that they are any better than anyone else or have a higher vibration.

For some Souls who contracted this virus, the message was for them to slow down. However, even after their experience with the virus, they still may not slow down and see the bigger picture. For other Souls that contracted the virus, a deep cleansing was moved through their physical vessel and in our eyes an upgrade in their Being.

No matter what truth resonates with you, this virus was the catalyst for an awakening within humanity. The only way this could have happened was by getting your whole world to stop for a period of time.

The virus will leave when humanity shifts into change and the dismantlement begins.

PREPARING FOR THE SHIFT

The following are steps to awaken what is important in one's life and what matters: Love, acceptance, and compassion to yourself and others.

Through the hardships that each of you will face, there will be a rise in resiliency. A knowing will arrive, that you are beyond your physical vessel. Honor and respect will occur for the physical vessel that your Soul is in.

To help with this shift, we recommend:

• Cultivating a meditation practice and bringing stillness into your daily routine. These two elements will bring clarity into one's life and an opening of awareness for your inner gifts to come forward.

• Every day, visualize Light in your energetic field that surrounds your entire body. Continue with visualizing Light around every human on your planet with the same energetic field around them. All of your energetic fields form the Collective Energy grid. This Collective grid is also within another energy grid that forms around your planet, known as the planetary grid. Now visualize the planetary grid surrounded by pure Light.

At this time, all three energy fields are rising in frequency and will rise even more with your daily practice of the above visualizations.

The new dawn is here with possibility, hope, and a new way of being. Old lands of new will emerge, new species will be discovered as the frequency shifts into a higher one. We are all connected through energy and energy is the way forward.

ENERGY FIELDS

Every living matter has an energy field around it. The human body has many energy fields around the physical vessel. Going forward it is important to take care of your energy fields and the human collective energy field. The majority of humanity is moving into the 5th dimension and with that is the mentality of oneness. Taking care of your energy fields and the human collective's energy field will greatly impact your planet's energy field. This is taking responsibility for your own energy as a species.

Personal Energy Fields

It is important how you treat your physical vessel with daily exercise, eating healthy foods and drinking clean, filtered water. One must also look after their personal energetic fields. Here are a few ways of looking after your energy fields:

1. Golden Light around your energy fields

This is done by visualizing golden Light around your personal energy fields, morning, noon, and night. In the beginning, try it for a few minutes with deep breaths each day. Set an intention for this bubble of Light to be surrounding you. Once this is part of your daily routine, you can begin to feel when the Light is in place. This can be done once a day or as much as you feel is needed. This visualization can help before going to work, school, and being out in public spaces where there can be many people around you.

2. Clearing your energy fields

When you are around others that drain your energy or you don't feel well in their presence, we recommend clearing your personal energy fields. You can do this by smoke cleansing, using palo santo, pine needles, or resins around your physical vessel, and setting the intention to release the energy around you.

Having a warm Epsom salt bath is another way to clear your personal energy fields, as is shaking and moving the body.

Shaking the body can be beneficial anytime throughout your day and when you are traveling as one might not have access to smoke cleansing or taking a bath.

To shake the body, place your feet hip-distance on the earth or floor. Keep your feet planted firmly on the ground, imagine roots growing from the soles of your feet into the Earth and stabilizing your energy. You can do this sitting or standing. Close your eyes and begin to gently sway your body like a tree, shake your arms and hands, moving your torso. Sway and shake for two to ten minutes. Notice how you feel afterward, as this only takes a short amount of time with a very positive effect on your energy fields.

3. Intention around your energy fields

Set an intention every day with how you want to feel and what you want to bring into your life. Through intention, your energy fields will strengthen. You can set an intention of love and an intention that your frequency is set to the highest vibration that is perfect for you each day.

Collective Energy Field

If every single person sent love into the collective energy field, there would be no fear.

That is what we are asking at this time, for a few minutes every day, for every human to *send love to the collective grid daily.*

To do this we recommend:

• Visualize an expansive field of Pure Divine Love and Light consciousness above your head.

• Now visualize a pillar of Light from this field of Love and Light consciousness entering your body through the crown of your head, slowly filling every part of your body. Continue to do this for a few breaths until you are lit up and surrounded with Light.

• Guide this energy of Light within you to expand out into your home, neighborhoods, communities, towns, provinces, states, countries, and the world. Continue for a few more breaths.

• Complete this exercise with bringing the Pure Divine Love and Light back into your body.

• Seal this exercise with sending Love and gratitude to the Divine field of consciousness.

With this exercise peace and calm will fill every human and will be felt throughout the planet. You will notice a lightness in your Being, as well as within your family and your home. The energy will flow through you with ease.

Planetary Energy Field

Each planet in the universe has its own energy field, within this field is its own planetary grid. This is the planet's signature, its identification. On Earth, there are access points within Earth's Gridlines, the ley lines, that offer portals for other species and Light Beings to be transported here. These ley lines are also known as highways for recharging space crafts. When the ley lines cross paths in the grid, this is an important juncture where portals can be created and openings to other worlds and dimensions can occur.

Other planets and the sun currently offer assistance in aiding humanity to awaken from their slumber of unknowingness. As the energy continues to shift there will be continued activity from planetary alignments, geomagnetic storms, solar flares, and Light downloads, all guiding and aiding humanity in their ascension.

For those that have been sensitive to the activity from the sun and Light downloads for quite some time, there will be a softening for you in the coming years to help aid others as they will feel the deep effects from the solar and geomagnetic activity.

DEATH, PRIORITIES & CHOICES

Death is the next topic we would like to address at this time. As mentioned before, there is no death to one's Soul. You are eternal.

It is the fear of death that will be eliminated. In the years to come joyous celebrations will happen when the Soul transitions onto the next part of its journey. It is merely a doorway from one life to the next.

Song, dance, food, and drink will be present at the Soul's celebration of transition and it will be looked upon with delight, such as other events like weddings and births.

It is a graduation, a stepping stone, a leap into one's journey to come to Earth and move onto the next experience, the next life.

The body that is left behind will be dealt with with the utmost respect and honor. There will be new technology that uses little energy for the human body to be recycled back into the earth.

Priorities

All inhabitants on Earth will go through a revamping of priorities. Priorities regarding their time, pleasure, and what matters most to them. Here are a few examples of what you may experience with the priorities in your life:

• In the years to come, you will know if you need to spend time on a project or move on from it. You will lose interest and forget about the project if it does not align with your Soul. If your Soul wants you to work on something, in particular, your energy will Light you up.

• The inside of your body will give you signs and signals when you enjoy doing something for pleasure. You will feel full of Light in the body and your chest will expand, filling you with happiness.

• It will become crystal clear what matters most to you and you will make this your top priority. You will flow with the energy at hand.

Choices

Every human makes choices that lead them down one path or another. There are no wrong choices. Every decision you make leads to experience and growth of the Soul in some form of your Being.

This is very important to remember that there are no wrong choices, for you are all learning and growing together.

This new way of being for the planet and humanity

will be one of simplicity as mentioned before. All systems will be revamped in one way or another.

Here are some examples of what will be unfolding in the coming years:

• The majority of post-secondary education will be online with teachers leading the students to enhance their abilities. This will not be the student teaching themselves but a new way of learning, specific to the child's energy and gifts. There will be mass elimination of subject matter that is taught today as this does not pertain to the new system of learning. Through technology, the student will have access to the teacher right in their own home and be connected with students from all over the world.

• There will be less travel for all. The Internet will be the way for meetings and gatherings with people that live afar.

• There will be other viruses that come into play which will also reduce travel.

• Celebrities will become obsolete as the majority of humans will spend less time watching TV and movies.

• The hierarchy of greed will no longer be as humanity balances the scales of wealth to be equally distributed to all.

• Individuals will look to the spiritual side of evolution and to spiritual teachers who resonate with them for upliftment and guidance.

• Where you live is where your food will come from. Almost all families with a yard or land will plant a vegetable garden to help sustain their family. Those that do not have land will have access to community gardens to plant their food.

• The financial system will go through an overhaul. Individuals will seek less borrowing from banks and eventually not rely on the pyramid scheme on which those institutions are currently set upon.

• A wonderful sense of community and looking after one another comes forward with the strength of love and compassion. Everyone will enjoy this new way of life.

• Vehicles that currently use fossil fuels will be a thing of the past. Living in areas where you can bike or walk to where you want to go will be the new normal.

• There will be new technology vehicles, new ways of transportation, and new forms of heating your homes without damaging the environment such as dams and mines that currently hurt and scar the planet.

• Mines, oil fields, fracking, and chemtrails will become obsolete.

Many events are happening behind the scenes that most humans are not aware of. This information would be too much for most to handle and would bring confusion to society. A severe shakeup would take place in people's lives as the majority are aware of one way of being. Certain steps need to be taken until the majority have awakened, then the information can be released.

Once this information is released, there will be a joining of forces throughout humanity for the highest good of all and there will be a return to how it once was.

All life is sacred, precious and should be revered. Currently, there is a group of species that have not respected the laws of the universe. Greed, corruption, and lies took over this group and manipulated all living beings. Some of this group was also wronged in other dimensions and were sent here unknowingly to bring chaos and control to this planet.

Know that there is both the Light and darkness. There is nothing you need to fight with the darkness other than shining your Light. The darkness has no ability to shine and diminishes among the Light. However, both are needed to experience duality.

At this time around your planet, there are many Starships and Light Beings that surround Mother Earth. These Light Beings, Galactic Masters of Light, and Councils from the multiverse are helping aid all forms of life and consciousness into a 5D reality.

Now is the time to work on oneself and release the layers of hurt, trauma, anger, and sadness. These feelings will not be present in the 5D reality. So, how does one begin to release these layers?

SOUL STEPS

Forgiving yourself and others is a progressive step to move forward into the Light. Part two of forgiveness earlier in this book is the first step. We recommend continuing and proceeding through with the following steps below as this will provide you with deeper freedom for the Soul.

Forgiving others

Make a list of everyone in your mind that brings up anger, judgment, or guilt. Examine this list, look at every name. Can you say, I love you, I release you, I forgive you? Look at this list every day until you can say those three phrases. I love you. I release you. I forgive you. It may take days, weeks, or months to do so. The amount of time it takes does not matter, what matters is that you can do it and you will become more liberated in the process. It is the dedication of looking at this list and the unfolding of release that will occur. Your energy will no longer want to hold onto the anger, judgment, and other negative emotions. Your Multidimensional Higher Self will want to move on and will be patient with you until you are ready to let go completely.

Forgiving oneself

How many times does your mind go through scenarios in which you could have, would have, or should have? All of these scenarios are part of the ego that holds your energy to the past. You have learned from the experience and it is now time to let those scenarios go. It is time to forgive and love yourself.

Place both hands on the heart and say to yourself, three times: "I forgive myself completely. I love myself completely. I let the past go. So be it and so it is."

You can take this a step further and write a list of all the things you would like to forgive yourself for. All the scenarios that could have been, would have been, should have been. Once this list is complete, find a safe space to burn the list. Once the fire is finished burning, a new beginning will be created.

There may be emotions that arise with these exercises, as it can be a long time in which those scenarios have been running through the mind. Once these exercises are complete, a sense of freedom and a new way of being takes place. Be patient with yourself because, with these exercises, there can be large releases in your energy field that can take time for your energy to integrate and reset.

SELF LOVE AND KINDNESS

To love oneself is to treat yourself as you would treat another person you love. Take the time to take care of you. Give yourself the love you deserve and bring joy and happiness into your life.

Be kind to yourself. Treat yourself with respect and have loving thoughts about yourself. Feel this love radiate into your whole Being. When loving yourself, you can feel your Light shine from the inside out.

As you begin to free yourself from your own personal shackles, you will be in the cocoon phase. This is the phase of inner work and perseverance. Once you have forgiven others and yourself, love yourself unconditionally and treat all others including yourself with kindness, thus the transformation begins. The metamorphosis of your Soul. The reemergence of who you truly are begins.

THE RE-EMERGENCE OF THE SOUL

In this step of the Soul, there is dedicated practice

each day in meditation or stillness. Most of your day-to-day interactions are mindful and set with intention.

There is a flow of synchronicities and events that will bring you into your Soul purpose and mission.

There is more happiness daily and confidence which grows in one's own self for dealing with your "stuff". You're seeing the difference in your life and the way you're following the flow of your energy and guidance.

You may not know what your Soul purpose or mission is yet, and that is okay. The synchronicities are leading you to where you need to go. Trust the process of the Light leading the way.

With millions of Light Beings assisting humanity, your transition will be less difficult than those that went through the re-emergence of the Soul many years ago.

You will be in a calmer, more observant state. If chaos surrounds you, look at it with perspective, strength and fortitude. There will be a complete shift in your demeanor. This does not mean your personality will change drastically. This means there is an energetic upgrade in your Soul wisdom.

TIMES AHEAD

There are times ahead that will seem as though you are watching a movie unfold before your very own eyes. The brain may not comprehend what is going on. We say this not to bring in fear, but to let you know and be aware of what is to come.

There are forces at play that have harmed humanity and other civilizations for far too long. Much will come to Light and the veil of illusion will no longer be. When the majority of humans are awake on your planet and all information is revealed, there will be a period of shock for most. The Lightworkers will need to take a rising stand in their mission and assist humanity. Many ways with how the planet once was, will change dramatically for the better. Here are a few examples of the times ahead:

• Money will no longer be of use.

• Traveling will no longer be on planes with recycled air. There will be machines that take you from one place to another, using zero fossil fuels and it will take half the time.

• Big box stores will be obsolete.

• Local products and local food will be kept in the area where it is grown and produced.

• There will be no more division between poverty and wealth. There is much coming into the Light about the wealthy and those that hold power. Many events that took place and continue to take place will be exposed for all to see. Light will be illuminated on these people and events, diminishing the negativity and darkness thus allowing healing to take place.

• There will be a continuous feeling of well-being as the vibration and frequency rise. The majority will connect with All That Is.

• As events will continue to unravel over the next few years, there will be lands and ancient civilizations that will be re-discovered.

• Technologies will advance using free energy and no human being will be sacrificed for bringing forward such advancements.

• Bills will be eliminated as water, heating and electricity will be free for everyone.

• Nature will be restored on Mother Earth, as the planet heals and becomes balanced. Humans will be aware of overpopulating the planet and respect the Earth once more.

• Communities will come together to take care of each other with food, supplies, and connection.

• There will be much less travel as mentioned before. Many Souls will be content with where they live and appreciate where they are located.

• As people advance in their development spiritually, their abilities will increase in astral travel and no longer have the need to see far away places on Earth. Through the mind and energy, possibilities open to other planets and dimensions.

STARTING WITHIN, CREATING YOUR DREAMS

To increase and rise in vibration, it begins from within. By working on oneself, your fears and doubts, releasing negativity, and forgiving all others and yourself, this can be accomplished.

Once you have done continuous work on yourself, there is a shift in your energetic bodies. Fears and doubts release, more positivity comes in and there is confidence in yourself and your abilities.

Through this confidence and strength that you have found and achieved on your own, your gifts and true self emerge.

This is an ongoing process to work on oneself. There is not one level to achieve and you are done. There are many layers to the Soul and learning about oneself and your unlimited capabilities.

When you begin to move through your transformations, you will also be able to manifest quickly.

Here are a few ways to help your desires and dreams come to fruition:

1. Intention is our first recommendation. Stating your intention and thinking about your intention is extremely powerful. You begin to align your thoughts with your deepest desires and the energy within that intention. Doubt, fear, and uncertainty can erase this intention. One must leave the fear and doubt at the door and with an open heart focus on the intention at hand. Believe that your intention will happen.

2. Write a list of your desires and your dreams. Keep your list in visible sight and look at this list when you wake in the morning and before you go to sleep. Vision boards are also helpful to bring your dreams to life. Many humans who create a vision board, find themselves astounded when looking back, as the majority of their vision has manifested. We recommend creating a vision board when your energy guides you to do so no matter the time of the year.

Through focused intention, without doubt, or fear, your desires will manifest. Once they happen, continue to make new lists, new vision boards, and dream bigger.

TELEPATHY, THE BRAIN & ENERGETIC BLOCKS

In the future, there will be no more phones, as you will be able to communicate telepathically to anyone across the globe. You will become hyper-aware of how to operate your mind and your mind will be in the present moment at all times. If you think of a person, immediately you open the line for communication. There are currently a small number of humans who can speak telepathically and many humans are beginning to understand the awareness of the mind. When they think of another, that person calls them or bumps into them.

There is much to discover about the brain. Your brain, as well as the rest of your body, is essentially a high-tech computer. When you treat it well, the possibilities open to infinite growth and expansion.

You see, there are signals in the brain that communicate between both sides of the brain. Every part is not yet utilized, however, as growth occurs this will change. Once stillness and meditation are a part of the daily routine, those parts of the brain which have been dormant will ignite. There is no need to worry about how this will expand or function. It will happen as you implement the previous tools in parts one, two, and three.

The brain has energetic pathways that connect to the spine and the rest of your physical vessel. Your body communicates with your energy bodies as well.

When there is discord from your past lives, these conflicts can attach themselves to this current lifetime. There can be an imbalance in the body, either physically, mentally, or emotionally.

An example of this would be if you have felt slightly depressed as far back as you can remember in this lifetime. You find out through a healing session that you were a knight in a past life in the medieval era. The family you swore to protect died on your watch, even though you did everything you could to try and save them. After that occurrence, you went into a deep depression in that life. The emotions and trauma carried forward into this current lifetime.

You may have wondered why you felt drawn to that particular era in time through movies or books.

Through past life regression, energy healing, channelers, and your work on oneself, these past lifetimes and energetic cords can be released.

As you move forward, it will help to make a list of what places you are drawn to and any specific time periods, as there is a likely chance you experienced a life in that time or dimension.

With this list, open up your mind. Are you drawn to science fiction movies or television shows? Perhaps, Angels, Unicorns, and Fairies pique your interest? Do you like the clothing from the 1700 and 1800s? Have you dressed up as an alien, an Egyptian goddess, or a mermaid for Halloween?

As you begin to open your mind in this direction, you may experience memories from your past lives. These memories or dreams can help you release what no longer serves you. Messages may come forward to help you in the present moment as the amalgamation of your former past lives begins.

With each past life you experienced, a piece of what you have learned has moved forward with you in this lifetime.

We would also like to bring to your awareness that not all of your previous past life experiences were good experiences. You chose certain life lessons and experiences to help the Soul grow. There were times in which you experienced deep sorrow, violence, judgment, and other traumas.

Releasing past energetic blockages is one of the keys to helping you bring balance to the mind, body, and spirit when the integration begins.

It is through releasing these past life experiences, that one frees the Soul from karmic attachment. To release these attachments, it is important to find a teacher, healer, or channeler that you resonate with to help in your healing. You can also do this by yourself through your own inner work, however, it will ease your process with the assistance from others.

It is also imperative at this time to sit with your emotions and to be alone with oneself to open and grow. Sit with who you are.

This may be uncomfortable at first and that is why one has kept oneself so busy. Many people have made their day-to-day lives so full of activities that there is no time to sit and look within.

This is why you are here: to learn and grow.

By sitting with oneself and allowing the fears, judgments, and emotions to rise, to sit with them and really look at who you are, this is progress. This is freedom.

Imagine being able to sit with yourself and enjoy being alone with no distractions.

Enjoy who you are and who you are becoming.

That is the goal.

IN THE BEGINNING...

Many eons ago, there was a decision to be made whether or not Earth and its inhabitants were to continue with the current hologram of Earth or to start anew and release all that was created back into the ethers.

There were Multidimensional Light Beings from all

over the multiverse that helped to create Mother Earth. When greed, corruption, and negativity took over, the decision was made to continue with the experiment at hand as too much had been planned and created to start all over again.

So the call for help was made, to bring in Light enforcements, and to tip the scales back into balance.

It was after the Second World War that the plan was to bring in a significant amount of Light to shift the planet and society. The darkness had overtaken too much in the world for humans and the planet to survive, there would soon be a tipping point of no return.

The cry for help reached out into the universes and there were waves of volunteers that would come through to hold and anchor the Light. These Wayshowers, Lightworkers, and Creators arrived, showing others that there is another way.

The first wave of volunteers had a difficult time with challenging ascension symptoms and deep emotions that were released from their own traumas. Many chose to end their lives as it was too difficult to be in the lower vibrational energies, however, they helped immensely with the time that they were here on Mother Earth.

The second wave are the ones who are helping humanity and Mother Earth ascend in this very moment. These gentle Souls are sensitive, generous, and hold deep compassion. There are layers within this group of teachers. The time is now, for all Lightworkers and Wayshowers to rise, teach, and aid Mother Earth and her inhabitants in the way that you feel called to.

The third wave are the Creators, they are the children now. These Light Beings will create a new sustainable way of living with advanced, free technologies to move into the New Earth.

These Beings will be open to loving a person whether they are female or male, as it does not matter the gender of the person, it only matters who the person is on the inside. This is the way moving forward for all humans, to be in a relationship no matter the gender, as you will be drawn to the person because of their energy and who they are in their heart.

The New Earth will have a more balanced life for animals, nature, and humans to coexist in a loving, sustainable way.

In the years to come, there will be more upheaval and breaking through the boundaries that were once set in place. The turmoil that many will experience will eventually be positive and turn into a deeper sense of peace and enlightenment of All That Is.

There will be more kindness and a deeper knowing that there is more to life than you are currently experiencing. All words for God, Creator, Christ,

Buddha, Allah, Jehovah, are all One. There will be a uniting of all on Mother Earth, a joining of Light forces through Love.

The walls of keeping humanity separate through their beliefs will be diminished. A feeling of gratitude and connection will be felt throughout all living Beings.

Yes, this is a grand experiment, and change is coming for all that want to move forward in Love and uniting with All That Is.

There once was a time of connection to all living matter on this planet. When greed and corruption took over Earth and changed the outcome that was originally planned, this too, changed the plan for the Multidimensional Light Beings who created this planet. That is what is happening to humans at this time. Be open to the changes that are now happening to your minds, bodies, and Souls. These changes are bringing back the connection to the heart and equal balance of the Divine Feminine and Divine Masculine.

The spiritual growth that will transcend humanity over the next few years is astronomical. That is why there are many Lightworkers present at this time.

Lightworkers and Wayshowers are the Wisdomkeepers that bring insight, clarity, and healing to humans. They do not interfere with another's life path or mission. They provide guidance into the unknown and with the help of Spirit, shift the population into the New Era.

The time is NOW to go within and release all that does not serve you, as the planet shifts into the 5th dimension. Souls that want to continue to learn in the 3rd dimension will remain in the 3D version of Earth.

Once the shift is made into the 5th dimension, most of the planet will not be the same as it is today.

This brings a smile to our faces, as we have been waiting for this moment for a millennium. There will be unity with the ones that are in the 5th dimension, and the negative emotions such as fear, worry, doubt, and concern will be eliminated.

One will know by simply thinking of the Light, meditating on the Light, and being One with the Light, this is what is needed to maintain a higher vibration and overall wellness to one's Being. This is what will occur in the 5th dimension.

This is the beginning of expansion, knowing that you are capable of anything, being anything you want and your desires can be manifested. In this vibration, the materialism and fame that are associated with the 3rd dimension are gone. There is no longing to be a celebrity, drive fancy cars, wear clothing that does not feel good to you, or support the planet. For this is an illusion and takes you away from your Highest Self.

In the 5th dimension, there is community, working together for the highest good and happy feelings through the mind and body. This will be a time of taking care of the Earth and implementing new ideas to sustain all life in a healthy and loving way. There will be a few years of 'clean up' on the planet and every Soul will have some part in this project. The air, water, and land will be cleaner and return to a more sustainable environment.

NEW AGE STAGES

This New Age will come in stages:

• Peace and kindness are recognized.

• Senses and gifts are activated and made known to oneself thus moving into a "Oneness" mentality.

• Clean up of the Earth and new technologies integrate to sustain all life.

• Awakening occurs with other dimensions and lands.

• Levitating, telepathy, and remembrance of astral travel become common.

As the planet begins to heal and cleanse, beautiful events will begin to unfold.

Rainbows will be common in the valleys and lands.

They will bring in clearing and healing to those that need a refill of energy.

Trees, plants, rocks, and minerals will have a glow of Light around them.

Humans will begin to reevaluate how they spend their time. As this happens do not be hard on yourself with negative thoughts. Humans are experiencing the most incredible shift known in all universes. This has never been done before at this velocity, going from the 3rd to 5th dimension while people are awake and becoming more aware.

Throughout the stages in 5D, Fairies and Elementals will show themselves. There will be laughter and fun once more. Life will be exciting and you will learn many new things. You will be in nature and connecting to All That Is, daily.

As humans begin to shift their awareness and increase their vibration, this will allow other Beings to enter the 5th dimension. Dragons will enter once again along with the Unicorns. Both of these animals are wise, peaceful creatures and will take the ones that are in the 5th dimension into higher realms.

The 5th dimension has its own signature frequency. At this level, there is a huge amount of growth in one's spiritual knowledge and advancement. This is one of the most joy-filled dimensions to be in as there is freedom in who you are as you awaken to love while being in a physical vessel.

In the 5th dimension, there is also a rising of energy in all that you do. The body responds to this higher frequency by living longer and looking younger. There are not as many ailments in the mind and body as the negative emotions do not exist here.

The 5th dimension holds Light and Love in a higher frequency than the 3rd dimension. With this Love and Light, you will attract a soul mate, without the use of the dating apps that you have now on Earth. No matchmakers are needed as you will FEEL who is aligned with you and who is not. There is a deep level of respect and honor with your partner and that alignment is held in the highest degree of Love.

In the 5th dimension, there is also a deep respect and honor for all life. There is especially an interest in listening to what others have to offer. The insecurity of having to talk to another when there is silence will be eliminated. For you will enjoy the stillness while being in the presence of another.

All life is precious and sacred. In the 5th dimension, an honoring of one's Soul, the uniqueness of who they are, comes to the forefront.

There will be timeline shifts as humans move into 5D. As the Light increases, one can bend time to their advantage, to help if more time is needed in an exam or if you're running behind to an appointment. Time will bend for you and in return, you will be able to channel the Light into your Being and spread it out into the world giving back with gratitude.

You see, energy is Light. Light is consciousness. Consciousness is All That Is.

We are all Energy, Light, and Consciousness. We are All That Is.

Once there is an understanding of your gifts, consciousness comes in and expands your awareness. This is the beginning of exciting possibilities and new adventures. This is where you take your life by the reins and create your reality. For you are your own creator.

Yes, there is guidance and support along the way, as you are never truly alone. However, there is newfound confidence that grows in your Being with who you are and what you have to offer. You begin to relax more and enjoy what is around you. You revel in being around others as they are being their authentic selves in return. You can now be yourself completely without judgment and ridicule.

The laws of the universe are simple.

We are all Divinely connected.

Be kind to oneself and one another.

Love is the key to all life.

This will be echoed out into the 5th dimension.

There is an opportunity for growth and expansion in the 5th dimension. There is also the feeling that everything looks a bit rosier, as this is what happens in the 5th dimension. You will feel the energy is different and not as heavy and dense as the 3D.

The 4th dimension is one of transition. Many of you now are going through the 4th dimension with seeing or integrating pockets of 5D.

In the 4th dimension, you learn to set healthy boundaries and, most importantly, who you can release from your life.

Who doesn't make you feel good? Who do you have a hard time being around and do not feel as though you can fully be yourself? This is the dimension to let go. This must be done to move into the 5th dimension.

The 4th dimension is the place where you learn to integrate the higher frequencies of the 5th dimension. This is a time when your body is also adjusting and changing to the Light.

There can be many ascension symptoms during this time and people will begin to wake in fear. Many will go to the doctor and wonder why they hear ringing in the ears, experience headaches and pains in the body. Some will feel pressure on their head or third eye, experience increased hunger, or have no appetite at all. These are only a few of the ascension sensations humans will go through as the Light increases and people begin to awaken.

Going through the tools of self-care will lessen the symptoms and help alleviate them if they reoccur.

THE TOOLS OF SELF-CARE

• Walking amongst the trees - spending time around trees resets one's own body, mind, and spirit, and helps ground the energy into your base chakra.

• Meditation - being in stillness, bringing the Light into the body, connects you with All That Is.

• Drinking alkaline water- this will help flush out any toxins that have built up from the increased energy waves and replenish the body with stabilization.

• Exercising - light exercise such as walking, yoga, Qi Gong or swimming will help move the energies through the body.

• Rest - there will be times of great exhaustion with the amount of Light increasing into the Earth. The body will need an additional amount of time to rest at different moments in your ascension.

As masses of people awaken, the time has come to join together, communicate with one another and feel what resonates within for you to move forward.

There are dark truths that have been played out for too long on this planet. The truths will now see the Light, to be set free for all to hear and know.

The time of awakening and change is here.

TIME OF CONNECTION

This is a time of connection, both individually and collectively. The blessings that humans currently have is technology, which keeps a global link with one another. Through this connection, information will be shared with all, to receive hopeful, positive knowledge about the occurrences around your planet.

Currently, corporations and tech giants have all the power and control. This will shift and their power will be no more in the years to come. This has to do with information coming forward that shows their creation of deception, power, and greed they have maintained. Once humanity awakens to the tipping point of balance, this is when these Beings will lose their power and be held responsible for centuries of old paradigms on this planet and galaxy.

When the majority of the population is positive and not focused on the mainstream media, there will be another shift. This shift is bringing awareness and understanding that what you listen to and pay attention to in your life, creates your reality and affects your energy.

Creating your world with positivity, being mindful of who surrounds you and what you listen to, will help create your reality with fulfillment, joy, and happiness. This is also taking responsibility for your energy.

As you continue to expand and grow, there will be less

attachment to outcomes, as all that is needed is in the present moment.

There are many worlds, dimensions, and species out in the universe and multiverse. You all have experienced many lifetimes and will continue to experience many more. These past lives may have been on Earth and on other planets as another species. Some of you chose to experience different forms on each planet, expanding your awareness, such as living your life in another Light form such as an animal, tree or mineral.

We want all to know that by being eternal, there is much to experience and enjoy within many different timelines, dimensions, and Light.

In each lifetime, the physical vessel that you are in holds a piece of your Highest Self. On Earth, there are many different shapes and sizes to a human body and letting go of the "ideal" perception of what one body looks like will be released as the world and energy continue to rise.

Enjoy the process of aging. With gratitude for your body, this can help shift your experience with how you live and love your life. With each year that passes by, it is another year to celebrate your experiences, growth, and knowledge.

LAYERS OF GROWTH

Let's begin to take a look at the layers of oneself in the ascension process. It is exciting to be able to experience each level and it does not mean that someone is better if they are on a higher level. Everyone is on their own journey of growth and has experienced and endured many events and circumstances in each lifetime.

There are many levels of growth. Here are ten levels to help differentiate where you are on your path.

Level one: In level one, you are sleeping and unaware. One goes along with society and its distractions. You are not aware of the spiritual world. The veil of forgetfulness surrounds you. You may eat heavier foods, party, drink alcohol, have a job that you don't like and you may feel stuck. You can feel like there is no way out and one may not feel fulfilled or happy.

Level two: In level two, awareness starts to slowly seep in. Events may trigger you to look at life a bit differently. There can be patterns that arise in one's life that you begin to look at and question. There is a small amount of expansion and less rigidity in one's life. A self-help book may intrigue you, and you may start to bring a little bit of exercise or movement into your life. You may help others once in a while, however, you can still have the feeling of being stuck and not going anywhere. There will also be moments of laughter and you may begin to notice the beauty of the world around you.

Level three: In level three, you begin to look for help. You start searching for ways to change and open up. This could include going to a therapist or a channeler and listening to their suggestions and guidance. You may begin to change your eating habits and start to bring consistent movement into the body. You may feel inclined to read more information on different topics expanding your awareness. This is the level where you are in the beginning stages of searching. Searching for what? More self-knowledge and growth within oneself and the Universe.

Level four: In level four, your searching starts to become consuming. You are a sponge for information. You may enroll in courses that intrigue you, you may travel and go to different places wanting to learn about other cultures and various ways of living and being. You will be reading books, watching documentaries, taking courses, and discovering who you are.

Level five: In level five, you are gaining perspective and opening the mind to what is happening beyond the veil. Awareness has opened to knowing that you are not alone in the universe. Your process has begun to work on oneself through forgiveness, releasing, clearing, and healing.

Level six: In level six, an awakening occurs for you. An awakening that you are here for a higher purpose to learn and grow your Soul. Your innate gifts begin to come forward and you are diving deep to learn about yourself through astrology, past lives, meditation, healing, and channeling.

Level seven: In level seven, you go through the layers of energy that are now affecting the body with the awakenings that are occurring.

Planetary alignments, solar flares, geomagnetic storms, Light downloads, and high solar winds are but a few examples of higher frequencies that you may feel throughout the body. You begin to look at self-care tools to help you through these times and notice the difference in how you feel when they are implemented and maintained.

Level eight: In level eight, you want to help others and you feel this deeply. You want to give back through service. This could be in a variety of ways: volunteering, teaching, donating money, offering pro bono services. There is a mindful awareness that we are all connected and you become aware of how powerful your thoughts are. Healing has taken place in the many levels of your Being and Soul and you are aware of the inner-work that needs to be released and cleared before fully giving back to others.

Level nine: In level nine, the synchronicities and signs happen often, if not daily. There is Love for All and a higher perspective is bestowed on all situations and events. Manifestation is occurring and you are aware that you are a part of Source. You can create and make a difference in your world and the world around you.

Level ten: In level ten, you are connected to All That Is. You are detached from outcomes and you know who you are as a Spiritual Being. You are an Enlightened Being. You are Creator, you are Source, you have merged with your Highest Self and the movement for Unity for All flows through you.

THE SOUL IN ASCENSION

Through ascension, acknowledging your fears and emotions, releasing these layers, this is what will help bring you into the 5th dimension.

When the majority of people are in the 4th dimension, it is time to create your New World for the 5th dimension and that time is now.

Right now is the time to imagine, write, draw, paint and sing your creation forward. Imagining technologies for cleaner air and a way to support all life on Earth.

Every single person on this planet has creative abilities. Imagine over six billion people (this is close to the number of people that will ascend) creating a future and dimension that is like no other in this universe. There will be millions upon millions of Souls wanting to take a turn in experiencing and seeing what you all have created.

It is also important to acknowledge, through Divine intervention, the many Light Beings within the Universes that are coming together right now, helping Mother Earth and her inhabitants through this ascension process.

When a Soul is born into a human vessel, that Soul has special gifts and abilities. When you are a baby, you see auras of light around each person. As children, you may have had imaginary friends that are your Angels and Guides. As humans age, the majority of these wonders disappear.

Some Souls can awaken earlier on in life and have a family that is aware and open to their gifts to help guide them. Other Souls that awaken early, have to keep their gifts to themselves as their family members or guardians do not understand or have the ability to be open in this way. This can be a lonely path with feelings of being misunderstood and not being accepted, however, it was agreed upon in their Soul Contract.

As each Soul awakens, it is important to tap into one's intuition, as this will bring awareness to one's ascension. It is taking notice of your body's reactions inside and outside of your physical vessel.

Do you feel shivers or tingles on the skin when your Guides are giving you confirmation? Are you aware of when you feel good or uneasy around certain people or places? What happens when you go with your gut feelings and when you don't?

The more you follow your intuition, the more guidance will come to you in a steady flow.

Your heart begins to open and healing occurs.

As your intuition becomes stronger, so do your innate gifts. There will be signs along the way to help you.

SIGNS TO HELP YOU

1. Colors - what colors are you drawn to?

Colors can show you what needs to be released and healed. This is not a black and white area. With colors, use your intuition and go through each color listed below. Do not read the caption beside the color, to begin with. Use your intuition and see what colors you are drawn to. See what resonates with you at this time. These colors do not represent the current chakra system. They are a guide to help you at this moment.

<u>Red:</u> Do you love wearing the color red? Do you surround yourself with red colors in the garden and home? This can mean you are a rock of strength for others. You are deeply anchored and connected to the Earth.

This may also mean you need grounding and connection to the Earth. You may feel insecure, worried about income, and may be in survival mode. If this is true for you, take the time to connect daily in nature. Nature resets the Soul and brings in grounding and a sense of calm to your Being. You will begin to notice a difference in yourself when this is maintained consistently.

<u>Orange:</u> Are you comfortable with your sexuality? Are you a safe haven for others and feel balanced? The color orange can represent confidence in who you are sexually and represent a balanced Being.

Do you have abandonment, sexual or emotional issues? Being drawn to the color orange can also be a sign to acknowledge, address and release these issues. If you feel this pertains to you, find the help that you need by talking to a counselor, therapist, or a past life hypnotherapist in releasing trauma and emotional issues to bring freedom to the Soul.

<u>Yellow</u>: Do you like wearing yellow? Do you see it on your walls and all around you? This can mean you know who you are. You have confidence and strength and your ego is balanced. You may offer innate wisdom by the way you show your authentic self to others and the world.

Do you have issues with not being good enough, self-doubt, fears, and anxieties? Being drawn to the color yellow may ask you to dive deeply into your fears and anxieties. As you release them, you will shine with more authenticity on your path, being true to who you are.

<u>Pink, Green, and Gold:</u> Does it make you smile when you see pink flowers and colors? Do you love being in a forest of green or seeing the colors of the leaves erupt when Spring arrives? Do you like gold jewelry, seeing the deep, rich colors of gold?

This can mean you are a romantic, love deeply, and truly love the Soul that you are. When others are around you, they can feel the love that radiates from your Being and out into the world.

It can also mean, when attracted to these colors, it can bring up heartbreak and wounds of the heart. It can bring forth a sensitivity so deep in the Soul that your heart is impacted greatly. If you feel this pertains to you, this is a time to heal the wounds of the heart and take care of yourself. Know your boundaries, give back to yourself and have compassion with truly loving who you are.

<u>Blue</u>: Are you drawn to the different shades of blue? Do you love looking at the sky with its soft colors of blue? Do you wear blue often?

This can mean you speak your truth, you can raise your voice when needed and you are not afraid to use your voice when helping others and those around you. There is power and freedom in speaking your truth.

This can also mean you need to strengthen your voice and say what you mean. Now is the time to speak your truth and release the fear that may come along as you do so. Many Souls on Earth have died using their voices in their past lives and this current one. Now is the time to release that fear. You are in a safe space of time. Let your voice be heard with strong, clear communication, and feel your Soul rise.

<u>Indigo</u>: Do you like deep blues and purples? This can mean you are highly intuitive and can connect with other worlds and Beings. The floodgates are open for information and messages to come through you from the Divine.

This can also mean a loss of connection to Source and your intuition. One may have doubts about your innate gifts. If this is the case, it is a time for meditation and stillness. Focus on bringing one's one thoughts in the positive and diminishing the negative thoughts of the ego.

<u>White</u>: Do you like wearing white? Are you drawn to white flowers, crystals, walls, and decor? This can mean you are connected to All That Is. You are Source, you are your own Creator and you are creating your reality.

This can also mean a disconnect in your reality and focusing too much on materialism, bringing in the illusion of fame and fortune. This is a time to see the bigger picture and to know you are much more than the physical vessel that you are in. There is more to the world that you are currently living in. This is a time to disengage from the material illusion and find out what brings you joy in the simplest ways and forms. This is an exciting time of learning and curiosity.

<u>Black</u>: Do you feel comfortable wearing black? Are you drawn to the layers and depth of this color?

This can mean you have not awakened yet and feel comfortable with not wanting to be seen. Black is not a negative color to wear, however, it can deprive you of wearing the colors of life that are all around you. Look in your closet and see how much black you have. Awareness is the first step and when you're ready, add the colors that make you feel good, showing yourself and the world who you truly are.

2. Numbers - are you noticing double-digit and triple-digit sequences?

Numbers have significant meanings and communicate that your Team of Light and Higher Self are guiding and helping you on your path. Take a look at the sequences listed below and notice throughout your day if these numbers come up for you.

<u>11:11 or 1:11</u> - 11 is a master number. Master numbers are high-frequency numbers that have powerful meaning and intentions. When seeing the number 11 this is letting you know an awakening is occurring and new beginnings are ahead. So ensure you stay on the path, all is well.

<u>2:22</u> - 22 is a master number and shows up when you are building and creating what is meant to be. Intuition and sensitivity in the Divine is rising within you. You are a natural-born leader with balance to offer the world.

<u>3:33</u> - 33 is a master number representing synchronicities and creativity. Certain events happen in three's for completion and lessons. These numbers are letting you know this is the case in a positive way.

<u>4:44</u> - 444 is a code from your Angels letting you know it may be time for rest and taking care of yourself.

When you see these numbers, smile for your Angels are guiding you.

<u>5:55</u> - 555 are powerful numbers to see in one's day. Your Higher Self and Team of Light are surrounding you and are cheering you on, as change and manifestation are taking place.

<u>666</u> on Earth has represented a negative energy of worship. However the number 666 meant something before it was misconstrued, it was the number of fertility and growth. 666 represents the Divine Feminine and this will be the way in the 5th dimension.

<u>777</u> represents the Divine Masculine. The number 777 is one of balance for all men going into the 5th dimension. All stereotypes and assumptions of the Masculine will be released with the number 777 and be brought forward into a heart-centered way of being. There will be schools and workshops in the future to help men with the balance of the Divine Masculine in love and acceptance.

<u>888</u> is the number of abundance and prosperity. However, in the 5th dimension, this does not mean money, fame, and success as it once did in the 3rd dimension. In the 5th dimension, 888 represents abundance in the heart, prosperity not only for the self but for All.

<u>999</u> represents the ending of a cycle. Seeing this

number in the 5th dimension can bring in joy, knowing all of your hard work has now come to an end as a new cycle is on its way.

Whenever seeing the numbers listed above, know these are Divine messages for you. Tune into your heart and ask what information these number sequences have for you.

3. *Nature* - Your Higher Self, Angels and Guides, and the universe, help you every day by sending signs and synchronicities of love and encouragement, especially when you spend time in nature.

Here are some signs in nature that may cross your path:

Hearts in rocks, leaves, flowers, the earth, and sky. The universe is letting you know you are loved.

Feathers, coins & rainbows can be signs from loved ones that have crossed over or can be signs from your Angels and Guides. These messages are ones of hope, letting you know you are not alone and to keep moving forward.

Seeing cloud formations can be another sign on your journey. You may see animals, Beings, Angels, Dragons, and Starships in the clouds. Use your intuition to what your Higher Self is telling you, as they can bring humor and guidance like no other, as they are a part of you.

4. Music - Music is incredibly healing and uplifting for the Soul. Music is a powerful tool that can calm the spirit and raise your vibration. Important messages can come across that will help you from the Higher Realms.

When listening to music, you can ask a question for your highest good and listen to what comes through for you. Use your intuition as it may not be the whole song that is the message but a word in the song or the feeling that you receive.

There are also pieces of music that have a higher hertz. This music will lift your vibration to higher levels. Explore music and sound for yourself to see what feels good for you.

5. Sounds - There can be sounds that alert you to pay attention before certain events take place. These sounds will vary from alarms, bells, tones, ringing, singing, and other sources. People around you may not hear the sounds, for it is meant for your ears alone. You may also hear sounds of upliftment such as singing from the Angels, Light Beings, and the Higher Realms, providing great peace and calm to your inner-being.

6. Animals - Animals, birds, and insects have a spiritual meaning when they show up in a human's life. For centuries on Earth, animals have been held in high regard as the messengers between the spiritual and earthly realms. Take notice when one crosses your path or comes to you in your dreams. Are you drawn to a certain animal in particular? Animals, birds, and insects can provide messages of clarity, hope, and strength. Use your intuition when one of these totems enters your life. You may be amazed at your own insights that come forward.

7. *Dreams* - Dreams are a way to process the subconscious mind and higher realms with messages to help you on your path. Dreams will be, more often than not, erased once one is awake. Keep a dream journal by your bedside and write down the dream as soon as you wake up. Ask your Soul for clarification with the dream and what messages you are needing to know in the present moment.

8. *Feelings and Body Signals* - Your energy bodies and energy fields communicate with you every day. These signs, signals, and feelings that you receive from your physical vessel are designed to help you in the present moment. They can be felt in many different states of emotions such as fear, anxiousness, joy, and Love. Here are some examples of the feelings, body signs, and signals that you may receive:

- Gut feelings such as a deeper knowing in your stomach

- Chills over the skin

- Hair rising on the back of your neck or arms

- Your whole body is on alert

- Heart racing

- Butterflies in the stomach

- Nausea

- Headaches

- Sweaty palms

- Heated face

- Heart expansion

- Tears of joy, happiness, or sadness

- Energy coursing throughout the body

These are signals from the body asking you to pay attention. Over time, you will begin to understand your own body and the alert signals to watch out for or the sensations you feel when you are in a state of happiness and joy. When you experience chills or goosebumps, this can be a positive confirmation from your Team of Light and Highest Self that they are with you in the room and/or the answer you asked is correct. It can also be an omen that you are on the right path. When you feel warmth in your chest and an expansion in your heart, this is an opening of love occurring with great magnitude that can radiate in your entire Being.

There can also be warnings within the body. When you feel you are on high alert, you may experience your heart racing and the hair rising on your neck and arms, and you may feel in your gut that something will happen. These signals you receive are EXTREMELY helpful and we advise you to pay attention to them.

When your palms are sweaty and you have a heated face, this can be a result of nervousness, anxiousness, and being put on the spot in front of others. If you experience this, you can communicate with your body that you are safe by taking a few deep breaths to calm your body down. Over time, you may notice that you do not experience these feelings as often.

These signals are here to help bring awareness for you to tune into your body and observe how much help you are receiving on a regular basis.

FEEL, LISTEN AND FOLLOW THROUGH with these signs, for they will never steer you wrong.

TEAM OF LIGHT, HIGHER SELF, ARCHANGELS AND ASCENDED MASTERS

Team of Light

Before you come to Mother Earth in human form, you have a Team of Light that has signed a contract with you to help you on your journey.

Your Team of Light does not usually consist of past loved ones. These Light Beings are from your Soul Group, Star Seed families, and Higher Realms to help you reach your purpose of why you are here. Some members of your Team of Light will stay with you through your entire lifetime and others will come in only at specific life lessons or junctures to help guide you.

Multidimensional Higher-Self

Your Multidimensional Higher Self (MHS) is the form of your Soul that oversees your life from the highest perspective. Your MHS will help guide you on your journey in whichever form you decide to take in all of your lifetimes.

Archangels

Archangels are Beings of Light that once were Angels themselves. These Light Beings have graduated into their roles and oversee Legions of Angels who are helping the masses upon Earth and other Realms. Archangels are teachers to the Angels and Wayshowers on Earth.

Ascended Masters

Ascended Masters are Beings of Light that have graduated from many, many lifetimes on Earth, and their role is to help humanity. Ascended Masters hold ancient knowledge and have first-hand experience of what it was like to live on Earth. Many Beings from the Higher Realms have not lived on Earth and do not know what it is to experience duality and polarity. Ascended Masters offer this gift to you. They are created from both the Divine Feminine and the Divine Masculine.

BIGGER PICTURE

To acquire knowledge and wisdom in your own life, it is important to have your own experiences. Through feeling and experiencing new things, your Soul opens up and continues to expand.

In the bigger picture, you are created with expansive energy and fit into a small physical vessel. Each human is extremely powerful with their own Light, Love, and intentions.

As each of you begins to see the bigger picture and recognize how expansive you truly are, a great amount of freedom is experienced, and knowing there is nothing to fear.

With each person shining brightly on the planet, all of your essences join together forming the most incredible Light in and around your planet. As the awakening continues, more Lights are being added to the collective daily. In a matter of a few years, there will be a noticeable difference in the Light that is shining within the Earth.

As the vibration continues to rise and TV and other forms of media fall away, there will be an increase in the creation of music in the world. This music will be channeled from the Higher Realms to keep your vibration high and bring enjoyment to the Soul. Many families will participate in learning how to play instruments together, sing melodies and harmonies, and bring fulfillment into their hearts.

Most of the music that is available on Earth will not be present in the years to come. This music has a lower vibration and was deliberately brought into the world with this intent. The same artists are popular over and over again, this will be questioned and the truth will be revealed. Throughout history and time on your planet, art, music, and dance of different cultures across the world have brought people together.

There is a new rising that will occur within this New Dawn. A creative burst of the arts will come forward once again on a much larger scale. People who thought they were not creative will find artistic expressions pouring out of them and will feel called to share their ideas and works for all to see.

This wave of creativity will be simplistic. Using and creating paints from the Earth. Writing and creating songs from the heart and higher vibrations. Dancing from the Soul without damaging one's own feet.

As the simplicity moves into each person's life, there will be more time for enjoyment of nature and the elements around you. This virus has shown many people it is important to slow down and take a look at what you have in front of you. Practicing gratitude and feeling joy for all the positive things you have in your life will help to support you even more. When one sits down and looks within, they will find the answer. This might mean leaving a relationship for you to expand and grow. This could also mean staying in a relationship, even if you are not able to share or see on all levels and aspects of life at this moment.

RELATIONSHIPS

The next few questions will help shed Light on your intimate relationships.

We recommend you read each question first, then answer from your heart and write down your answers. These questions are meant to bring your awareness forward without fear. For it is your choice to continue or leave your relationships. When looking back at your answers, explore them with curiosity and love in your heart.

Trust

1. Having trust in your partner is of the utmost importance right now. *Do you trust your partner completely? Why?*

Love

2. Love for your partner is the second most important step. This love is not the roommate kind of love.

We ask, are you IN love with your partner? Do you genuinely like to spend time with your partner? Are you proud of your partner, the person, and the Being they are? Why?

Commitment

3. *Are you committed to your partner and are they committed to you? How are they committed or not committed to you?*

Passion

4. *Do you have passion in your relationship?*

Passion can be very strong at the beginning of a relationship and this can also change after many years of being together. This is natural for humans. Passion can take on different forms later on in the relationship with feelings of deep respect, trust, and love throughout time and your experiences together.

Take notice the next time you are intimate with your partner. Do you feel passion, trust, and respect for one another? Take the time to sit down and truthfully answer these four questions. They can help you move forward in the relationship or let it go completely so you can experience all of these wonderful attributes with a loved one when you are ready and the timing is right. These questions plant the seed to take a look at your relationship in greater detail with your partner. Relationships can be complicated, cause struggle and hardship, or they can be as easy and fluid as you want them to be.

FAMILY RELATIONSHIPS

The next few questions will help you in your family relationships and dynamics.

We recommend going through each section and answering each question from your heart.

Unconditional Support and Love

• *Does your family love you unconditionally and support you wholeheartedly?*

The family you are brought into may not have had the tools and awareness to provide you with love and support. At this time of ascension, an awareness of awakening within you arrives to take a deeper look into your family and the love and support they provide for you. For those of you who have experienced support and love from your family, bring in recognition and gratitude to them for providing a strong family base in your life.

For those of you who have not experienced this, it is time to cut the cord with these relationships. As you speak up for yourself, there may be a time in the coming years that your family members awaken and seek forgiveness and reconciliation.

This can be a challenging situation letting go of loved ones and setting healthy boundaries.

By listening to your heart and releasing the family relationships that no longer serve you, there is a warrior within that stands for your right to be happy and free.

FRIEND RELATIONSHIPS

The next few questions will help you in becoming aware of your friend relationships.

Read each question and answer from your heart. You may be surprised when you take the time with your feelings, which truths come up that have been concealed or hidden.

• *Does your friend judge you or love you unconditionally?*

• *How do you feel when you are with your friend? Do you feel uplifted or depleted?*

• *How does your friend treat others and yourself?*

Having people in your life that you trust and lift you up is essential at this time of ascension on your planet. It does not matter how many friendships you have, only if they are true and authentic to you. Some friends will come into your life for a short amount of time and others will be with you for an eternity.

No matter how long the person is in your life, trust that the relationship served a purpose at the time, either in Soul lessons, compatibility, or Love.

SOUL GROWTH

As each Soul awakens, there will be an accelerated wave of lessons and Soul growth that each human will experience.

In the previous years and centuries, one Soul may have decided to learn one to three life lessons in the span of a lifetime.

At this time and in the years to come, there is an accelerated advancement in Soul growth. This has to do with the energy that is being implemented on Earth and the Light that is intentionally being transmitted from millions of other Light Beings.

The outcome of this shift, going from the 3rd dimension to the 5th dimension, will have a great impact on many planets and Souls throughout the Multiverse.

In the human body, lessons are being integrated within days and weeks at a rate that can be challenging to comprehend to the mind, body, and Soul. As ancient knowledge and awareness become available with the continuation of shedding the layers, so too does the Light begin to rise in your Being. As this transformation continues, we recommend allowing the emotions that arise to move through you. For many people, there can be moments of tears, depression, and breakdown. In turn, this can shift to feelings of anger, pain, and frustration that lead to a rising motivation within you. When the dust settles, there will be a lightness within you and a new perspective of the world.

These moments of transformation will continue to guide you to a greater life and light force, which enables you to move into the 5th dimension. This is the only way to move to the next dimension. With the accelerated rate, there will be moments that bring you to your knees, transforming you into a new version of yourself.

For some of you, the transformation will be more physical. Feeling this in your vessel as layers are released through your entire Being. Others will feel this more emotionally. They will be going to the depths of the darkness and shifting into the Light. Experiencing moments of doubt, confusion, lack of confidence, and instability. When these moments occur, it is time to go inward, to journal, to breathe, and know this WILL pass once the layers are shed. As each layer is released, trust becomes more embodied. Trust in oneself, trust in the Universe, and trust the energy at hand. This energy guides you to opportunity, abundance, and prosperity. There will be shifts into the new and letting go of the old. Releasing old patterns, letting go of materialism, and the outdated ways of thinking. Community, intention, and genuine kindness to one another will lead the way. New ideas and thought processes will begin to enter the mind. Your past lives and previous gifts will come forward and merge with this current one, helping others and this planet.

As previously stated, there will be Souls that will not want to move forward at this time. They will not be ready or want to move to the 5th dimension and beyond. They will take leave in ways that were pre-planned in their Soul contract before entering the planet. Trust that you will see these Souls again when your body leaves this planet.

These Souls can be family members, friends, and acquaintances that are in your circle now. Honor where that Soul is. Do not despair that you will not see them again or that they will not be in your life in the future. Death is merely a doorway they have gone through to continue the lessons and Soul growth in the dimension they have chosen.

The bigger picture for all Souls on Earth is to fulfill the contracts and Soul missions that were laid out before you which you agreed to before entering this planet. If on any level you feel these are outdated contracts, it is but an intention that one sets to clear this. Setting your highest intention to align all your contracts now for the highest good of all and All That Is.

HOW TO FULFILL SOUL CONTRACTS AND SOUL MISSIONS

Each Soul signs a contract of the lessons and experiences they want to learn before entering this planet.

Within a Soul contract, there are multiple timelines that one can take to achieve the lessons learned.

You will know when you have learned a lesson when you think about a situation or person and you feel differently without being triggered. In each lesson, it is a circle in which you will continue to repeat or call in similar people and situations until the lesson or experience is learned.

When a human or other life form can not easily see the writing on the wall, this can lead to the manifestation of disease in the physical vessel. This is not negative, nor should one beat itself up for not seeing the red flags.

Your journey is one of growth and expansion. Be kind to yourself as you are always learning.

Once the Soul lesson is learned, there is a lightness that arrives in your Being, and awareness is brought forward to the layer(s) that are released.

Each Soul has a mission to fulfill in this lifetime.

A Soul Mission is a purpose. It is the reason why you are here.

There are different times in a Soul's life that your Mission is activated in your Being to be completed.

There is a drive that comes with this Mission. Perseverance will help you find out why you are here and the drive to forge ahead will help you follow through with your purpose.

Trust the process that you will be shown the way to your purpose and the timing will be right for you no matter where you're at in your life.

The less you compare yourself to others and focus on your journey, the more aligned you will be with your Light.

Many of the Lightworkers who are here on the planet at this time have a Soul mission to bring their Light to help shift the planet into a higher dimension. Part of their lesson can also be in teaching others.

To teach what they know, what they've gone through in their own experiences, and how to trust their energy, being their Authentic Selves as they shine their Light from within.

Many Souls are on different levels and will need a variety of teachers in this lifetime. If you are a Lightworker, your guidance is needed. Some Lightworkers will teach in smaller groups while other Lightworkers will teach in larger groups or one-on-one. You are needed no matter what size the group is that you teach.

All missions have one intent: to complete their task at hand and to move into their next mission in the next lifetime. All missions have been worked out with your Highest Self, your Team of Light, and the Light councils.

You will feel you are on the right track when completing your mission when there is lightness within your Being and you maintain a consistent level of happiness.

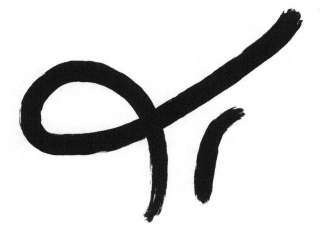

AUTHORITY

Currently on Earth, governments and law authorities rule and govern your planet. This will change as the planet and humanity continue to rise into the 5th dimension. Change is at hand and there will be significant transition occurring in the years to come. This transition is led by hope and inspiring change in people's hearts. This positive outcome will be coming very quickly, as it has already begun.

People will begin to speak up and support one another in heart-centered ways. The old ways of bullying and singling people out using shame and ridicule will abruptly come to an end.

As people band together, governments and law authorities will have no choice but to move with the people. Yes, there will be disruption and chaos in the coming years, however, it will ultimately lead to peace. Peaceful chaos to transition the majority into the new.

There will be less need for law enforcement, as the Souls that do not want to move into the 5th dimension will remain in the 3rd dimension and disruption will remain there.

There will be much change in the coming years, releasing the old ways, bringing in new ideas for communities to thrive and for all people to be treated equally. The color of your skin, gender, or sexual preference will have no effect on the new way of Being.

The old way paradigm, the old rules, the old way of Being, cannot exist in the 5th dimension. Control and secrecy will be no longer.

Greed and the affluent will be no longer.

Starvation and the poor will be no longer.

A balancing of the tide is coming and long overdue. The Lightworkers are rising, holding, and maintaining the Light at such a frequency for all humanity to shift.

Yes, there will be an uprising as it brings in the change for the new way of Being. It will be led from the heart, for all to share equally, for this is the way forward.

This new way of Being may seem far beyond the mind's reach for many right now. Each Soul will begin to see this new way of Being as layer by layer of the old begins to become dismantled.

There has been a lot of information being held back from humanity from those in power for far too long. There is currently enough wealth and money on Earth to treat all humans and Souls from sickness, ill-health, and poverty. As the transition continues, this information will be coming forward. All cancer can be treated, all diseases can be treated, all mental illnesses can be treated. The disease in one's body comes from not addressing certain issues in your life. Cancer is an emotional disease that can be cured by getting to the root of the trauma or blockage that needs to be released.

Babies and children that are born with a disease, sickness, or mental illness have agreed to help either their own Souls, their parents, families, or caregivers to expand in their Soul expansion within their Soul contracts. They wanted to experience life on Earth no matter how short their time was. This can be heartbreaking to lose a child or loved one when they are so young. It can feel like this happened for no rhyme or reason.

There is a bigger picture here: one of healing, strength, and endurance. Over time, the heart heals with the connection made from the other side as they help aid in healing and understanding.

DISCREPANCIES

In the years to come, there will be discrepancies that come forward. These discrepancies will show you in your heart what needs to be released. They are meant to be felt individually. If you are with a partner, friend, or group of Souls, this is a journey of one's own heart. We recommend not to follow the path of others and to follow the path that is meant for you.

When seeing and feeling these discrepancies, we recommend using your discernment. Tapping into your intuition, your gut feeling, and connecting with what resonates with you.

We advise all, to look at everything, absolutely everything in your life with discernment. You will know in your heart if the information sits with you correctly.

As you begin to see and feel these discrepancies in your Being, there will be more balance in the Light of your Soul. This paves the path ahead for an easier way forward as you will see these discrepancies clearly over time.

You may ask, what are discrepancies and what will they be?

Discrepancies are versions of truth that will be presented to you.

An example of this is the news. You're watching the news one evening and they report one "fact" to you. When you see this message, your heart and energy may stop for a second and you think "Hmm, that doesn't seem quite right." Later on that evening, you sit with the message and you feel in your heart that the "fact" is not true, as all truths were not shown.

You realize by tuning in with your discernment, there is a discrepancy within this "fact". This can lead to confusion, as many Souls begin to unplug from the matrix.

What do you believe? What is real?

This is where all the previous teachings in this book take effect. The tools in this book will help strengthen and bring awareness to the connection you have had along: the connection with your heart.

THE 5TH DIMENSION

Imagine a world where everything is balanced. You awaken each day to excitement, curiosity, and freedom in who you are. This is the 5th dimension. In the 5th dimension, all are equal, life is balanced and each Soul is connected in community.

Love and Light shine in and around your Being every day.

Every Soul will have a roof over their head if they so desire.

Every Soul will have access to clean water and food daily.

Every Soul will have its basic needs met as a human.

This is where Mother Earth and humanity are now headed: into the 5th dimension.

Listed next are elements in society that will change in the 5th dimension.

Schooling

There will be a variety of schools for children and their gifted abilities. All children will learn a new way of Being, spiritually, with how to treat others and how to treat your planet.

Each child will go through certain tests to see the level of their abilities, which would send them to the school of their choice.

The tests that the children will go through are nothing like the ones Souls went through in the 3rd dimension, where there was only one way of learning and one program to follow. These tests are universal, as they are used all around other universes to help the Soul reach its ultimate goal of learning and growth.

Schools will be similar to what you might have seen in science fiction movies on Earth. Smaller groups of children being taught by a Master(s) of those lessons and abilities.

Once children have reached a certain age, they will be moved into an apprenticeship program. This one-on-one schooling will give them the confidence and courage they need to move into the position or job they desire.

There will be no cost to go to school and further your education. There will be a planetary system put in place that all Souls will be provided for as money will no longer be a necessity.

Population

As Mother Earth and Humanity move into the 5th dimension, this dimension will remain on Earth for centuries to come. There will also be fewer humans on this planet.

Right now, the population is affecting the planet at a detrimental speed and Mother Earth has gone beyond her maximum capacity of Souls living here at one time.

There is a certain number of Souls that can live on Earth which is beneficial for the planet. Those numbers will be maintained in the years to come with no grievance or uprising from others as all will be connected to the health and prosperity of the planet.

Homelife

Homelife will be similar to what it is now in regards to family and pets being at home. What will differ in the coming years is the quality of life.

The Souls that have been overwhelmed and kept their lives busy will go through the biggest changes. There will be a shift in their energy and awareness that one will not need to fill their calendars with one activity after another, leaving no quality time for family at home.

Eating, cooking, and spending time together as a family unit will be the new normal.

Creativity such as art, playing music, singing, gardening, and other artistic activities will occur daily.

When children are young, they need to spend time with their imaginations, spend time in nature and be with other like-minded friends of their own.

In the 5th dimension, there is a sense of peace with safety for all. Parents will allow their children to play outside unattended at certain ages for there will be no Souls that will abduct or kidnap your children, as this vibration will not be present in the 5th dimension.

There will be more community gatherings and help for all in the areas that you live in. Self-isolation will be a thing of the past. Happiness, joy, and a personal sense of fulfillment will be achieved daily.

This is what we want you to know: the 5th dimension is one of peace for families and all.

Work

The jobs and work that you choose will be one of passion. There will be transition and movement in each job if so desired. Many of the jobs that are now on Earth are ones of monotony. The same experiences over again, day in and day out.

There will be a variety of different jobs and training that one Soul can learn and continue to grow from. Once you have achieved a level and awareness in that job, you will have the option to move on or stay in the same position and teach others.

There will not be corporate or CEO jobs in the 5th dimension. The 5th dimension is one of working together for the collective and all Souls are to be treated equally no matter what job you choose.

Imagine a time where money is no longer an issue and you can do whatever it is you dream of to help others, to help the planet thrive, and to help your Soul grow to its full potential in this lifetime.

The 5th dimension is one of possibilities, growth, and freedom while being in the physical vessel.

PHYSICAL VESSEL

The body you are currently in has never experienced a transition such as the one humanity is now going through. As the energy shifts and transforms each of your bodies, you will notice a few changes that occur over the coming years.

There will be a youthfulness as some of you age. Your skin can have a light glow to it and you will look a certain age for much longer.

The body will not need the heavy, dense foods that many are currently consuming. This process will evolve, with the collective changing as the frequency rises. This brings awareness to all, shifting what is available in stores, markets, and shops around you.

Food is fuel for your vessel and it is important to enjoy delicious food for the senses.

Taste is a wonderful sense to experience while in your body in the 5D. There will be many new creations of food dishes and many varieties of fruits and veggies that will come into fruition in the near future that attain to the senses.

The body will be leaner as more Light enters the body and increases over time. There will be fewer aches, pains, and ailments as the body will be a well-oiled machine, working at a high capacity with the quality of fuel that you are providing.

THE MIND AND EMOTIONS

Your mind will be much clearer in the years to come and there will be more focus in the present moment while in the 5th dimension.

As the Light increases, dormant brain synapses will be activated and there will be less primitive ways to communicate. You will be aware of how powerful each and every thought is. When you think of a person's name, you open the line of connection with them, either through telepathy or in your dream world.

With the mind becoming clearer, so too do your emotions. There is a level of peace that you will enter within the mind when one is in the present moment.

Imagine all of the frustrations that are on Earth now: the sensations of anger, jealousy, doubt, and worry, all being eliminated as you will have shifted in letting that all go. Once this comes to the forefront, you will not want to go back to experiencing those emotions again.

COMMUNITY

Within each community, there will be a coming together which existed centuries ago.

In the years to come, there will be an energy that flows

through neighborhoods, towns, and cities, transforming the old ways of thinking and bringing forth a fresh new start.

This new start brings in open communication with one another. Taking care of those who are in your circle and your community, takes on an energy of its own. Your heart will be full and there will be joy in talking to one another and conversing.

Without the distractions of the media and the TV, there is time to prioritize for one another. There is time for celebrations with food, song, and dance.

What was happening on your planet with self-isolation went to such an extreme and it was harmful to humankind. To be away from your loved ones near or far is detrimental to one's own mental health and well-being.

On a positive note, the self-isolation with the virus will soon come to an end. New information will come to Light and break down the barriers those in authority have put up. This self-isolation was also a call to wake up, which was the catalyst that needed to happen so that humanity could go within.

ADVANCEMENTS

New technology advancements are coming forward with ways to clean the planet and sustain all life in equilibrium.

Once the information comes to Light in the coming years, there will be a time of transition, a time to go within and integrate. This is not a time to jump to the next level and become enlightened. After this process of absorbing and integrating the new information, then comes the new ideas.

These new ideas are advancements in your society.

These advancements come from other solar systems and galaxies that are proven to work at lightning speed to recalibrate the air, water, and land which were originally pristine millions of years ago.

This period in time will be a unification as a species, with the drive and purpose to clean the centuries of harm to the planet. All of the Souls that are in the 5th dimension will contribute to helping Mother Earth.

PEACE

Peace is a feeling of calm in the heart, that all is well in your Being.

Many Souls on Earth in the 3rd dimension have not experienced long lengths of peace. Perhaps moments of peace, however not prolonged periods at a time.

In the 5th dimension, there will be peace in your Soul.

To achieve peace, there is work that needs to be done on oneself with releasing the layers of trauma, the boundaries and confines of society, judgements and views from others and yourself.

It is taking responsibility for your own Soul. No other can do this for you. With this work and releasing the layers, comes what all Souls want: true inner-peace. Peace in the heart and peace in your Being.

ELEMENTALS

In the 5th dimension, elementals will show themselves once more.

In the beginning, this will be energetic. You can close your eyes, sense and feel them, these wonderful Beings of Light.

As the cleaning of the planet moves forward and healing begins in society, the elementals will come forward to help those who need to experience joy. There will be laughter, curiosity and deep remembrance.

Elementals are keepers of the beauty and nature around you. They bring in laughter, silliness, lightness of character and fun to all those that surround them. Elementals truly are magical creatures that have chosen to be here at this special time in the 5th dimension and beyond.

LANDS

In previous tales and books centuries ago, there were stories of lands that held healing properties. Lands that many traveled from afar to see and experience.

In the 5th dimension, these special lands will be acknowledged. They will have special healing properties in accordance with the Earth's ley lines. There will be dedicated Souls that will look after these lands and healing areas.

We want all to know, the entire Earth is healing. This acknowledgment will rise once again in all humans, once the truths are revealed and integration takes place.

These sacred sections of the Earth have been known to other species for some time. These species come in crafts to recharge their ships with the energy that is potent in these sacred spots.

Some humans are aware of these areas of land. We want all to know there are many areas that have not been revealed, due to the density of the planet. These sacred sites have been protected and will be revealed when the shift into the 5th dimension is complete.

The sacred sites have a higher energy and can speed healing and light frequency in each Soul. These areas will only be accessed when necessary and can pertain to different circumstances with each Soul.

The caretakers of these sacred areas will meet and convey information to help each other stay connected and share information within the collective. Their role can be passed down from one generation to another if the Soul desires this to be.

PORTALS

There are portals on your planet that currently exist to go from one dimension to another. Some of these portals are not accessible due to the dimension and chaos that is surrounding Earth as you all move through this 5D transition and transformation.

Once these portals are open, there will be curiosity and excitement for each Soul. There is nothing to fear, for there will be teachers who come forward with the knowledge to help others pass through the portals when they are ready. These teachers will have guided information that will come to them when the time is right.

Each portal moves into a different dimension for Souls to experience new lands, meet new Beings, and open the mind to the vastness of the universe.

CRYSTALS

On Earth at this time, there are only a few crystal caves that have been discovered. We would like you to know there are thousands of crystal caves and tunnels on Earth as we speak.

These crystal wonders will be revealed over time and they will not be harvested to be distributed. The crystal caves and pathways will be enjoyed by many to explore, bringing in a reset to the Soul and awe of how incredible your planet truly is.

In the 5th dimension, there will be an emphasis on crystals and how beneficial they are. Some Souls are aware of this information, however, the majority of the population is unaware of the assistance crystals can give you.

Crystals are living Beings that hold a Light frequency. The energy of the crystal can reach thousands of kilometers away from its original location.

Crystals need to be charged and tended to. They like to be cleansed in the sunlight, full moon energy, and crystal clear water from the Earth. Some crystals will deteriorate in water, so ensure you take the time to research the crystal you have and see which ones can aid you as you need them.

Crystals can also be programmed to hold a certain frequency and memory.

In the years to come, there will be large crystals in the center of healing rooms and temples. The majority of homes will have crystals in them and people will carry crystals with them.

TUNNELS AND SOUND CHAMBERS

Over the centuries, humanity has lived in the Earth. Tunnels and passageways were created to survive as a species when the elements above were too harsh for humans.

These tunnels and passageways are all over the planet and have been buried and covered by cities and towns that have since been built over them. There is ancient wisdom and teachings in these tunnels and passageways that will be revealed over time.

Within some of these tunnels, there are sound chambers to ascend one's vibration to a higher level.

Some of these chambers have been discovered but not utilized as they once were. This is what will occur, people will begin to use these sound chambers to raise one's vibration. These will also be used for healing. The vibration of the sound moves through the entire body and shifts the frequency, thus creating harmony in the cells, and instant healing occurs for many.

There are also access points to Middle Earth deep within some of these tunnels.

MIDDLE EARTH

In the center of your planet, there is another world. This is called Middle Earth.

Middle Earth holds DNA codes of all life that have ever been on Earth. This is sacred information and has been securely protected from forces that seek to harm others.

Middle Earth holds the energy of a very high vibration and has plant, fauna, and animal life that has not yet been seen with human eyes. Middle Earth will permit access to the explorers, the Souls that will venture deep within the Earth to share this knowledge with others once the vibration is high enough on Earth.

Middle Earth is not a place to fear. It is one to protect and hold sacred. The energy in this world is of such a high caliber that many will want to take the journey to experience this for themselves.

STARS AND PLANETS

As the shift in frequency rises, new star systems and

planets will be shown to Earth.

These planets will be shown to all in the years ahead. They will be seen through devices such as telescopes, however, they will be much larger and with greater magnitude and clarity than the ones that are used today.

These star systems have been hidden and obscured from human eyes. Divine intelligence protects sacred knowledge from the 3rd dimension and all forms that live there.

Light Beings from these star systems helped create, in partnership with humans, the temples that you have now on Earth. The pyramids in Egypt, the Mayan temples in Mexico to Brazil, the chambers in Argentina, the stone walls and structures in England, Ireland & Scotland. These structures were not possible without guidance from these Beings. They hold the energy that was adhered to by many and new structures will be built and advised from the star systems once more.

The purpose of these structures is to enhance information and knowledge to one's Soul. They are gathering places for Light-filled ceremonies, higher purpose learning, and community gatherings. There are also portals and chasms within these structures to move through to re-enter another part of the world.

GALAXIES

Within each galaxy is a solar system. Each solar system has planets and star systems. Many of the planets and star systems are habitable.

There are thousands upon thousands of galaxies within your universe and there are billions of universes within Source.

We share this knowledge to open the vastness of the multiverse within your mind and to remember and acknowledge the many lives you have experienced upon different star systems, planets, and galaxies.

TRANSITION DIMENSIONS

There are dimensions in this universe that are known as transition dimensions.

The 4th dimension is one of transition from the 3rd to the 5th dimension and so is the 6th from the 5th to the 7th dimension and the 8th dimension from the 7th to the 9th.

Transition dimensions are dimensions that have staggering learning curves for each individual. When a planet such as yours goes through such a transition, millions of Souls line up to partake in the experience to grow as a Soul.

These are planes of frequency that allow a transition period to realign your energy from one dimension to another, it's like stairs in a home from one level to another. You need the stairs to get you to the next landing or you would not be able to accomplish getting to the next level.

There are certain qualifications when applying to go through a transition dimension.

Qualifications:

• The Soul has experienced a certain amount of lives and Soul growth to be able to participate in this next phase.

• The alignment within the Soul must be present to help for the highest good.

• A deep knowing that each Soul will teach in some capacity after their energy crosses over from that lifetime. They will teach other Souls their perspective to help those see if they are ready to partake in such an advancement.

DIMENSIONS 5, 7, 9, 10 11, 12

We would like to state what each dimension is like at its core level to give each an understanding of the lessons and growth that can be achieved within each level.

5ᵗʰ - As the Souls enter the 5ᵗʰ dimension, there is a greater love and compassion for all. Awareness of your Light comes forward with the capacity to grow and align your gifts.

7ᵗʰ - The 7ᵗʰ dimension is for the Angels. You may have experienced a lifetime or many lifetimes in this realm. In the 7ᵗʰ dimension, the purpose is to serve others with your guidance, Light, and understanding. The ultimate goal at this level is one of service, giving back, and providing hope to all. Love and Light prevail over all materials, matter, and outcomes.

9ᵗʰ - The Souls that are in the 9ᵗʰ dimension are ones with deep knowledge. They are the creators and manifestors. In this dimension, the purpose is to teach others through their wisdom.

10ᵗʰ - The 10ᵗʰ dimension is in crystalline form. This is pure energy that radiates into the Souls, the planets, and the galaxies they are in. There is a holding of the Light in this form and vibration.

11ᵗʰ - Councils are in the 11ᵗʰ dimension. There are many different areas to oversee, guide, and direct in its highest form. The Souls that are chosen to be on the councils have experienced life in each dimension and are here to serve in this capacity.

12ᵗʰ - The 12ᵗʰ dimension is in its highest and purest

form of Light within this universe. In this dimension, there are no physical bodies, it is pure energy and pure Light. The purpose is to create the highest form of energy, thus enabling access to the multiverse.

In all of these dimensions listed above, there is a pure state of Being. There are no attachments in the physical sense of emotions which the 3rd dimension offers. This is also why many Souls are wanting to participate in this great awakening, as they want to experience the polarity of your world.

In the years 2020 and 2021, the transition began for the Lightworkers to release the old and step into their roles to be of service to humanity in the years to come. In the 5th dimension, there will be no going back to the old ways. Souls that are on the waitlist to come to Earth will also be of assistance with bringing in change and advancement to the new world. These Souls will not be able to experience the full spectrum of 3D as in the past.

As all Souls look back on their time on Earth, they will realize how fortunate they were to experience this profound lifetime of cleansing, releasing, and healing.

THE YOUNG ONES

The babies and young children currently on Earth are the Souls who carry information that will transform into the New World. Some of the parents of these little ones have been in awe at the profound wisdom that comes from these Souls.

Their gifts will manifest quicker and more prominently than Souls previously born in 2012.

In ten years, the way children become educated will be unified. In the years to come, children will be able to experience the way school is taught upon similar planets among many other species.

ORBS AND SPHERES OF LIGHT

Orbs and spheres of Light will begin to show in the 5th dimension. Currently, you can see orbs of Light and spheres when looking at a picture you have taken.

These special Lights can represent fairies, Angels, Light Beings, the Divine Feminine, and Divine Masculine energies that surround you, letting you know they are with you.

In the coming years, when you see these orbs of Light, this will bring confidence and happiness into the heart and Soul. These orbs are at a higher frequency and love to be surrounded by nature, sunlight, and joyous events. That is when the orbs will be present and show themselves to you. It is a gift and honor for these special

Lights to be seen.

Spheres can appear in many different formations. They have Light codes in them that will transform your energy into a higher frequency. When seeing spheres of Light in the future, you will be able to stand under them and receive the Light codes within minutes to upgrade and clear your energetic body.

Through time and space, these spheres have come to help assist humanity.

OPPORTUNITIES

There will be opportunities that will arise for each human during this evolutionary shift. These opportunities are ones of self-growth and advancement, as you all move towards the 5th dimension at lightning speed.

Each opportunity will present itself as options. For each human, the circumstances will be different, however, it is in the questions that you ask yourself that will determine the opportunities at hand.

We will break this down into a few examples to show how some of the opportunities will appear.

Example 1: You go to the coffee shop and you see an old friend sitting there. You have the option to go over and say hello or you have the option to pretend that you didn't see them, grab your drink and leave.

You are presented with two choices.

Option 1 is going over and saying hello, it may have been an immediate action in walking over and being in the present moment.

Option 2 is not going over, there could have been hesitation in your energy and the feeling of not wanting to say hello.

Ask yourself the question after the fact, why did I go over and say hello? Or why did I not?

The options above are examples of energetic awareness. Honoring how you feel and moving where your energy leads you.

We are merely showing you from now and onwards, there is a shift in the energy, and a big shift in the Light. These examples of how you react and feel in different situations can change. Pay attention to how you feel in circumstances and who you are around. There will be a time of no longer hiding who you are as the frequency rises. Also, there will be an adjustment in your energy as you move into different situations and events in the coming years. Trust your energy and the options that are presented to you.

Example 2: You debate whether to book the same practitioner again. This could be a hairstylist, massage therapist, counselor, healer, etc.

Option 1 is to work with them again, even though you did not feel satisfied by their work, however, there is a sense of loyalty to them.

Option 2 is you choose to go with someone else. With this new person, you feel confident in your decision and happy with the outcome at hand. The silver lining in this option is that you are allowing your energy to guide you and you let go of all attachments.

Ask yourself the question, why did I book with them again or why did I not? What is the result of doing so?

In this example, there is awareness of letting go of expectations and attachments, for when you do, there is a flow of energy that will move through you. Letting go of the worry of hurting the person's feelings and letting go of what is not yours. Once again, you are in the present moment, where anything can happen. This example shines Light on why do you feel loyal to someone when they don't meet your expectations or provide the service that you want? Paying attention and bringing awareness to this will help your energy and your decision-making moving forward.

Example 3: You've been invited to a party and you've accepted the invitation. On the day of the party, you do not feel like going.

Option 1 is to go and follow through with your original decision. In Option 1, there can be pleasant surprises in meeting new people and supporting the event, person, or occasion and this leaves you with the satisfaction that you proceeded with your commitment.

Option 2 is not going ahead with the invitation. There is no right or wrong here, simply another outcome. With Option 2, there can be satisfaction with your decision as you were not ready to partake in the event, however, a curiosity might come up with what would have happened if you did go.

Ask yourself the question, did you make the decision for yourself or was it out of obligation?

What we want the collective to know is that it's important to tap into your intuition. You do not have to say yes to everything and the same goes with saying no. Your immediate reaction when receiving your invitation will never steer you wrong. Your immediate reaction is in the present moment and that is what we want you to take away from this.

Even if you don't follow through with your immediate reaction, your energy will lead you where you need to go. Eventually, you will see or feel the signs that are presented before you.

You always have options. When you feel you're at the end of your rope and there's nowhere else to turn to, there is always another way.

There is always hope, guidance, and above all else, your powerful intention to move forward and find the next option that will present itself to you. The Light is here and will continue to rise, showing you the way.

CONNECTION

Your Soul is connected to all living things. As each human on Earth and the collective moves toward the 5th dimension, so too does each Soul's understanding of how each one plays a vital role in the equilibrium of the planet.

This understanding will come in time for each one of you. Everything is connected: the land, the air, the water, and each living, breathing Soul.

Once the masses of humans begin to flip the light switch on and each Soul becomes awakened, so too does the connection with All That Is. This connection becomes stronger, effortless, and resilient.

The connection that we speak of does not pertain to one between humans, this goes much deeper than that. The connection with All That Is is with EVERYTHING and this is not as overwhelming as some might think.

For example, think of this dimension like the ocean on your planet, and all the living creatures and the humans represent what's in the ocean. What is occurring and happening in this dimension, affects everything in the ocean.

This is what you will find with each one of you. Everything that is happening in the 3rd dimension on this planet is affecting every Soul on some level. However, when moving into the 5th dimension this will affect you and everything in an enlightened way.

It has been long overdue for the hidden truths to come forward from the 3rd dimension and to move into a state of healing and equality for all.

Now is the time for each one of you to focus on yourself. Each one of you holds the key to your self-growth, expansion, and learning. All of the distractions that are surrounding you are keeping you from your own potential.

As you work on yourself, this changes the frequency in not only your energetic fields but the energetic field of the collective and the planets. You have huge implications on the energy within All That Is.

We say this now as time is running out to bring to your awareness, what is at hand. To work on yourself and to move into the 5th dimension. This is not based on fear or premonition, we bring this to your attention as we are speaking the universal truth.

UNDERLININGS OF THE SOUL

Each Soul has already made the decision to move into the 5th dimension or remain in the 3rd, this decision was made in your contract long ago. We want all to know there is no Soul left behind. No Soul needs to feel alarmed with where they are going.

Your existence is based on growth and making these

decisions for yourself was done before entering your life here on Earth. Now is a time to trust where you are at, let go of fear, attachments, and outcomes.

When you do this, the flow of the universe, the Divine, moves with you. It is a wonderful process to be able to trust the Universe completely and this is that time, right here and right now. You are partners together.

With each Soul contract as we've said before, there are other Souls, Guides, Helpers, and Angels that commit to helping you in certain moments as you experience your Soul lessons. They are not able to interfere with leading you down one road or another but will offer guidance and support, showing you many signs. However, it is up to you to be open enough to see them.

Through time and space, there is the infinite, the vastness of knowledge to all. It is up to each Soul on how you want to learn, grow and move forward.

Each Soul is Energy, each Soul is Light, each Soul is Love. The human vessel that you are currently in is one of many "suits" that you have been in over your lifetimes.

Some of the same Souls that you had other lifetimes with are currently with you now. You will recognize the Soul in the way that you feel about them. You may feel as if you've known them for a long time, as there is a connection, a cord that links you to one another. You might have even experienced a physical reaction when seeing them for the first time. Being around their energy can be very magnetic.

What we advise all Souls at this time is to pay attention to how you feel around certain people. How is your body reacting? What signs is your body giving you?

With the reactions that you receive, honor your energy and body by following through with how you feel.

BODY REACTIONS AROUND OTHERS

Tiredness

If you feel tired after seeing a friend, an acquaintance, or another human, this can be a sign they are taking away your energy. These Souls can be energy vampires and they may not be aware they are doing this to you. They do know they feel great after seeing you, and for yourself, you may need to take a nap after seeing them to recharge. Ask yourself the question: do you want to be around someone that depletes your energy?

Physically Sick

If you feel physically sick after seeing another or find you are verbally fighting with them, this is a large indicator to stay away from this person. Your body is giving you physical symptoms on how your energy is reacting. If you proceed to be around this person, your body may continue to get sick. We highly advise you to take caution and provide space around energies that make you feel sick or cause highly charged emotions.

Fearful

If your body reacts with fear, the hair rises on your arms or the back of your neck, or you have a sinking feeling in your belly, these are signs to stay away from this energy. There is a danger to your Soul and we highly advise you to take leave from this person. If you are not able to get away, call in your Team of Light, your Angels, and Guides, your Highest Self to protect and help you. Listen to the physical signs of your body, as this can save your life and are lessons in Soul growth.

Protective Stance

If your body moves into a protective stance where you move your shoulder and arm to protect the heart and belly, this can be a sign to protect your energy from this person. Your body is automatically shielding your energy to help you. Be aware of the communication your body is giving you, take a deep breath, and remove yourself from the situation.

Happiness

If you feel full of Light and happiness when seeing a person, this person can be in alignment with your energy. They take no energy from you and you take no energy from them. You can lift each other up when needed and your heart feels happy after seeing them. This is balanced energy and will be felt in the 5th dimension with all Souls.

OBSTACLES

As Souls transition towards the Golden Age, over the next few years, there will be obstacles to overcome as a society. There will be a definite division of Souls that will remain in the 3rd dimension and those who are moving into the 5th.

The obstacles we speak of are of human nature itself and the instinct to reach out and help others. This obstacle will be between the 3D humans and the 5D humans. There will be no war or conflict, but a heartache of sorts to overcome and release.

Once the transition is complete between the dimensions, there will be a flow of energy and movement within the 5th dimension. The obstacles that you once faced in the 3rd dimension will no longer exist. You will have a higher perspective, a different view of how life is and why you are here. There will be no deceit, no shame, and no wondering if the other person in the 5th dimension has an alternative motive. For you are all in this together, learning, growing, and expanding.

For those of you that are reading this, you will be the ones that are going into the 5th dimension. There will be fewer interactions with those that are not awake and choose not to be. This is not an ignoring of those Souls but an awareness on an energetic level not to participate or try to help them understand as they have chosen to continue to learn in the 3rd dimension.

As a society, there will be many layers that will be uncovered. Healing will need to be done and then released for the karma and cycles to be broken.

There will be groups of Souls that will come forward and volunteer their services to help aid in the healing. Their Soul purpose and their mission will become known to them as they awaken. This wave of volunteers is awakening now into their roles as administering the healing for humans and the planetary grid.

At the same time in which this wave is waking up, so too will another wave of volunteers who will wake up to their Soul's purpose to the restoration and regeneration of life. This is a longer pathway for these Souls. There will come a time in the very near future when there will be access to Middle Earth and the DNA codes that have been protected and hidden throughout time. These codes will be released and given with much appreciation to the Souls that will work and support the regeneration of Life.

Through technology, science, and experimentation (not on animals or human life), there will be success in bringing back plant and animal life that was once lost to thrive among humans once again.

EVER-FLOWING AMOUNT OF LIGHT

The 5th dimension will take you into quite a different time and space than the one you are in now. There will be an ever-flowing amount of Light that surrounds you and is available to you in many facets of your life.

The physical Light you see from the sun will be brighter and there will be an adjustment period after each Solstice on the 21st of December.

We have mentioned earlier that physical bodies, rocks, trees, and plants will radiate a soft glow. This is your inner Light shining through. Some of you, you will see this sporadically over the next few years, until this is the new norm.

There will come a time when most people will become aware of their chakras (energy centers in the body) and which ones need tending to. There will be Chakra Healers that will help balance your chakras and release the attachments in the years to come. By tending to your chakras and maintaining their frequency, so too does this impact your Light's radiance and the quality of Light you emit.

Within your Light, there is guidance. This guidance is from your Multidimensional Higher Self, your Angels and Guides, and their wisdom to help you along your path.

This is an exciting time to enter as the 3D comes to a close for many. This transition period of awakening brings forth the teachers that are now moving into their roles to aid the humans that need help.

Within each of you lies the unlimited capacity of Love and Light. Over the next ten years, there will be a time of growth for each individual. Self-love will be a theme and the acknowledgment that One Self deserves Love and you are worthy.

The journey of self-awareness will be specific for each person. This will be the most challenging part for many, as they release the demons which have long plagued the masses and awaken to your spectacular Light.

The teachers that will come forward will bring in a sense of ease and help you attain your commitment on the path that lays ahead of you.

SOUL'S PURPOSE

As each individual awakens, a sense of needing to know your Soul's purpose will come forward. For some, it will feel all-consuming.

Listed below are a few categories of Soul purposes on Earth at this time. Read below and see how your body and energy react to each purpose. You will know your purpose by the reaction you have and know this may only be one part of your mission. If you're still not sure afterward, take the time to inwardly ask the questions.

Bridges: Souls that are Bridges bring in information from one realm to another. They are the connecting piece that is needed at this time of transition. Bridges can be channelers, psychics, healers, shamans, counselors, therapists, and energy intuitives.

These Bridges have a constant connection to the Divine and the Cosmos and can have an overwhelming sense to serve others in this way as they relay information to help Souls ascend.

Transmuters: Beings that are transmuters are Souls that physically take in the negative, 3D energy and vibrations, transmuting this within oneself into the Light. Some of these Souls will go through physical pain. These Souls need to seek the practitioners that will release the blockages from their energy fields regularly, as this is essential to their well-being.

Being a transmuter is a huge job in the bigger picture. It is not an easy task to take on this role. It can be a lifelong journey dealing with the pain and sorrow of others until the Light has increased to a level where the discomfort no longer affects them.

Beacons & Anchors: Beacons and Anchors are Souls that have volunteered to allow the Light to pass through them. The Light then anchors into the Earth and stabilizes the Light that radiates out from them. With these Souls, their Light will affect a room, calm people down and make others feel relaxed just by being around them. They are positive Souls that have a high frequency to allow large quantities of Light to move through them. These Souls can be extra sensitive to the higher frequencies and Solar Activity that moves through your planet. It is movement, rest, and self-care that is needed for these Beacons and Anchors to help them through.

Ignitors: Ignitors are Souls that ignite other people's purposes and gifts. These Beings are clear channels that will release blockages for others and help to activate other Soul's Divine and innate gifts. Their evolution is very quick. There are not many igniters on Earth so one of their purposes is to teach to groups and the mass collective.

Earthers: Earthers are Souls that have experienced many lifetimes on Earth and other planets tending to the animals, plants, soil, and the general care of the land. Earthers are essential for the well-being of Earth, and in turn, affect all that reside on the planet.

Earthers love to garden, be outside in all seasons, and enjoy all-natural facets of life. The purpose of Earthers is that through their Light they send a vibration to all living life and matter that grounds the energy around them into the planet they are living on.

Templates: These special Souls are the experimenters, the ones that take a risk into creating different solutions to see what will work for the highest good. Through technology, science, and creativity, they formulate an equation with Divine Light to serve humanity into a higher consciousness.

These Souls love science, books, and learning. They like facts and search for newer, better ways to help and advance their world.

Miners: Miners are Beings that do not originate from Earth's galaxy. These Souls are selected from other solar systems. These Beings are the ones that will go into the depths of the Earth when it is time to explore the crystal tunnels and caves deep within your planet.

Miners are not like the ones you currently have on Earth. These Beings are not here to mine crystals or destroy the Earth. They hold a higher frequency and a layer of special cells that allow their skin to glow deep within the Earth, which protects them from the elements of different gasses and humidities.

BEINGS OF LIGHT TO HELP ASSIST HUMANITY AND MOTHER EARTH

During humanity's ascension over the next decade, there will be Beings that come to assist Earth and her inhabitants. This information is not to cause panic or fear to anyone, as these Souls will only present themselves to those who are ready energetically.

Wavers: Wavers are created from the Light. These Souls will come down into the Earth's atmosphere in the years to come. Wavers are Light Beings that use telepathy and hold a higher frequency to change the ionosphere of your planet and bring back what once was by repairing the damage. Wavers send out waves of Light Energy that increase the energy fields and transmute any stagnant energies of decay and rot.

Elementers: Elementers are the woodland folk, the guardians of the elements, the keepers of the Earth that will once again show themselves as they once did long ago. They will help to repair the planet and will provide education to humans. Elementers will teach the ways of the land, how to respect and honor the planet and teach others how to communicate with the plants, animals, and trees.

Star Seeds: All humans are Star Seeds. We all come from Source and each one of you has experienced other lives in other Star Systems in other forms. We speak of a particular group of Star Seeds, who are among you now and many of them are the way-showers and teachers that are helping assist humanity in this ascension. This group of Star Seeds are Beings of Light who help seed planets. All Souls are created from the Light, however not all take on this mission of seeding other planets.

There will also be other Star Seeds that come from afar to help humanity. They will show themselves in their crafts and communicate to others through channeling until the frequency reaches a vibration where they will be able to show themselves to all.

Dragons: Dragons are of the higher realms that come with guidance and assistance to the elements. This next step for humanity is one where the Dragons will assist at a much greater capacity than ever before. A Dragon's frequency is of a very high vibration, not only will the human standing next to them feel this but the entire vicinity that surrounds them. You will know when a Dragon is in the area for your acute awareness increases and you will be on high alert. Not in the sense that you will be in danger, as this high alert is one of your acute senses. You will become aware of the bugs in the air, the dust in the room, the Light, everything slows down for you but the energy is running at a MUCH higher frequency. Each human has the ability to connect with the Dragons as they rise in ascension. Dragons have ancient knowledge and offer fierce protection from those that seek to harm others. Humanity must also realize Dragons can not be called upon whenever the human wants. Dragons help those with a pure heart and clear intentions.

Unicorns: Unicorns are Source's Divine creatures of the Light. These special Beings are one of pure Light. They offer guidance to those in need and provide comfort and solitude for Souls with troubled hearts. Unicorns prefer the quiet and to be in nature as they enjoy peaceful solitude away from others. You will find these serene, peaceful Beings when you call out to them in nature and they will come to you in your mind and heart. Be patient with these Special Beings for they do not come at your beck and call. They will arrive on a wave of gentle, soft purity. Unicorns offer the purest of hearts and Love in the Soul.

Transformers: Transformers are Light Beings that convey messages to the other realms and Beings on how Earth and her inhabitants are doing with their transformation in dimensional shifts. These Beings are dedicated to informing other races with the Highest Light and knowledge to improve others' experiences and life force.

Transformers will go from planet to planet, universe to universe, observing and cheering behind the scenes on the progress and advancements of the planet they are on. In a way, you could think of them as a group of auditors on planet Earth. As they observe humanity's awakening, they share their information of the highest and purest quality with other Light sources that are suffering or in need of this knowledge.

Light Contributors: Light Contributors are Light Beings that will station themselves at certain points and places around your globe. With their contribution of Light to the planet and the masses of other Light Beings, Earth will transform itself into health, beauty, and vigor, how it once was eons ago.

Light contributors are specific to their role. They are here to solely focus on bringing their Light in and allowing the Light from the other Light Beings that surround your planet to move through them thus anchoring more Light into the planet. They are similar to the human Anchors & Beacons on your planet.

Pacifiers: Pacifiers are Light Beings that subdue the energy around them from conflict to peace.

Pacifiers do not work out the problems at hand but aid in calming the energy of all parties. They do not take away what is to be solved or worked out at the moment. They aid groups and leaders of their communities with their energy for an outcome of peaceful resolution.

When a Pacifier enters a room, the energy shifts to one where the tension ceases and all parties can take a deep breath.

Pacifiers will be needed to help humans resolve long conflicts of war and ancestral issues in the DNA of one's own memories.

Star Lights: Star Lights come from Light years away to help Mother Earth and humanity open up their Light capacity within each of their Souls. These Beings will come to humans in their dreams and while they are daydreaming, providing information and questions on why you might be thinking a certain way. They provide a new way of thinking for expansion if one is feeling stuck.

Star Lights help assist Mother Earth by providing her Light support in the ascension. These Beings will focus their intentions on sending Light into Mother Earth's core helping her move through this birthing process into the 5th dimension.

Star Brights: Star Brights are smaller Beings of Light that move from realm to realm assisting the elementals. These special Lights are not fairies. Their primary purpose is one of service, pure Light, and movement.

Fairies also hold the Light and can be full of fun, play, and mischievousness. Fairies prefer to stay in one area, assisting the fauna, plants, and living matter in their environment.

2020 AND BEYOND

Before fully moving into the 5th dimension, there will be many channelers and healers that come forward. As there are over 7 billion people on your planet at this time, there will be masses of people looking for assistance and will need information to help ease and soothe their Soul.

Many humans will be sponges, looking for information until they find their own way of knowing the answers themselves and move into the new way of Being with All That Is.

The new way of Being is a way of feeling through the heart. Listening to yourself and what feels right to you. This will be automatic for all to feel this, to know what is right for you, and feeling the Light that has been pouring down on all since the shakeup began in 2020.

The transition from the year 2020 and onwards will be different for everyone.

For the way-showers that have been on the awakening path for a while, these Souls will move further into their roles as teachers, paving the way for others to ascend into the Light.

For those that have just awakened, there will be a period of adjustment. This is the time to be kind to oneself and to have patience as your awareness unfolds.

For those that are still sleeping, there will be Light events that happen in 2021-2025 that will awaken these Souls if they have chosen to move into the 5th dimension.

Fear not for your loved ones, family, and friends if they have not awoken yet. There will be no one left behind that does not want to be. Both dimensions have lessons and Soul growth for each individual. We want to advise all to not get caught up and focus on whether your partner, family members, or friends will awaken.

Each Soul has chosen what they want to learn and the majority will move into the 5th dimension. Respect and honor the decision of the Soul that does not "wake up". For they are not ready and may not want to experience the 5th dimension yet. Remember, the majority of the population will shift.

The day the Veil of Light lifted on the Solstice,

December 21st, 2020, was the day the Light shifted the energy where every crevice, nook, and cranny of darkness that was hidden will be exposed to the Light in the years to come. There is now an enlightening path opening for humanity. This event will not change everything overnight, however, it will be looked upon as a new beginning, an enlightened age of the Light.

After 2020, change will begin. More Souls will awaken and all will see the change coming to the Earth. For those who are awakened, they will also bring their ideas to fruition.

Just as December 21st, 2012 was a cosmic event with all twelve chakras being activated in humans on Earth, so too did December 21st, 2020 draw the line in the sand for the New Dawn of Light to enlighten the majority of humanity.

What we would like to clarify is that this new age will take time. This will not happen in a year or two. The key is to work on one Self and as you do, each Soul goes through its own awakening process. This process is not a single event. It is a series of steps that one must take and each step will be completely designed for each person.

EQUALITY

There has been no equality within humanity for centuries. Women, children, people of color, and minorities have been sacrificed and used in horrific ways that have been hidden from the masses. Now, truths will be revealed and it may take time for humanity to wrap their minds around such events which will come to Light.

One of these concepts is the belief that there is one Universe and one God.

There are billions of other Universes within All That Is. A Soul can be a Universe.

This can take a moment to absorb. Within this universe that we are all currently in, there is not only one God. There are two, a Creator and Creatrix. A God and a Goddess. There is the Divine Feminine and the Divine Masculine which creates a union of Love which is the core of All That Is within all Universes.

This is not to say that it can only be a human male and a human female in their partnership together to create this Love. We are talking about the energy of the Divine Masculine and the Divine Feminine within each Soul.

You will notice if two males join together in partnership, one of the males may have more Divine Feminine in their Soul than their partner who has more of the Divine Masculine.

This can be the same for two females in a partnership, as well as a female with a male. The human male is not all Divine Masculine, just as the human female is not all Divine Feminine.

Each Soul has both energies, the Divine Masculine and the Divine Feminine inside of their Being. It may not be of equal proportion, however, there will be both inside.

Now moving forward in the years to come, there will be a remembrance of the Divine Feminine in all essences of your Soul, whether you associate with being female, male, or gender-free. The Divine Feminine is coming back to equality as it once was.

There will be balance once the remembrance has come to fruition. Love is the core of all Universes.

This information of there being a God and Goddess within your Universe has been covered and hidden from all for centuries.

Why has this been done? The forces at hand took over the balance of Light and Dark and burned, hid, killed, and tortured into submission the ways of Truth. Many of you will know this in your Being with your past lives of being burned at the stake, being killed, or tortured. You may feel an aversion to anything on your wrist or neck. You may not enjoy dark and confined spaces. You may not like being too close to fire or have a fear of drowning. You may feel shame when having sex and not understand why you do not like being in certain positions.

These feelings and fears are related to what has happened in your past lives and also in your current life. In the years to come, as humanity moves into healing on many fronts, you may remember a memory, a feeling, an experience of your past lives and previous deaths to heal the Soul. This is not to be feared as you will be ready energetically when you do experience this and will have the tools at hand to help you navigate. Our channeler Sarah experienced one of her previous deaths in Atlantis while on a canoe trip. She was camping in the wilderness as a storm came in with high winds, torrential rain, and lightning. This created the remembrance of Sarah's life as a healer and her final moments in Atlantis. Waking up for Sarah in the tent on that howling night, brought in the memory of her being swept away by a landslide from a massive wave and hanging on for dear life to a tree as her world crumbled around her. This memory of trauma that Sarah had been holding onto unknowingly brought in the awakening and healing of her Soul's energy from that specific lifetime, propelling her forward in her life's work in this lifetime. This remembrance was very traumatic to Sarah but needed to happen to release the energetic block.

Not all Souls will have to relive each lifetime of trauma. However, there will be many that will experience some of their past lifetimes to help their Soul, energy, and their life purpose.

There will be Light healers and Light coaches that will be able to help you through these experiences if needed. Remember, you will only experience this when your Soul is ready.

REMISSION

Remission will be a period for all Souls that will happen after the truths are exposed and the planets and humanity's energy goes through healing. After this takes place, there will be time for all to be in a state of remission.

In this state, there is an alignment for each Soul to partake in Gaia's healing within her Being. It is a time to restore faith in humanity and all Souls. This is where Love expands and grows. This state of Remission will happen for many in the mid to late years in the decade of 2020.

THE TURNING OF THE TIDES

As each Soul moves through its transition and communities band together, the Golden Era will begin. Being in this transition can be overwhelming for some and others a time of anticipation.

As each Soul turns inward and works on itself, the information will come forward that your inner knowing will never steer you wrong. This critical piece of knowledge will serve you in the years to come.

Your energy will let you know when it is time to see a friend or let them go from your life. When you feel drawn to be in a certain place, location, or store, you will feel the pull, the need to be there.

This is the turning of the tides that we speak of, going within and listening to your inner guidance.

It will not be loud and abrasive. It will be subtle, gentle, and ever so loving. You will feel excited when you are lit up with an idea and feel an ever need to move forward. Possibilities will be endless in opportunity.

Abundance will be ever-flowing to all.

Society will break the chains that have been wrapped around them for centuries. So Dear ones, we say to each one who is reading this: Be patient with the outcome at hand. Your new world will not happen overnight, as this new era will be unfolding for centuries and you have only just begun. Know in your heart that each of you has an important role to play. This role is either to help awaken those around you, bring in new technology with your ideas and innovations, or to hold the Light which is moving into the frequency of the 5th dimension.

OUTCOMES

This next part of the book is about outcomes in the years to come. These outcomes will pertain to the breaking down of current institutions such as religion, churches, corporations, CEOs, banks, governments, schools, health care, and Pharma care. These institutions have all been strategically built upon lies and deceit to the public under the veil of illusion.

As the truths come out, that is when the deeper healing for humans will begin.

Church and Religion

The falling of the church and religion will be the first and the utmost biggest change in your society. It is the corrupt way in how it all began centuries ago. You see, the seed was planted that with faith and a belief in a god, a religion, you will go to heaven if you are "good" and "well-behaved" or to hell, if you are "sinful" or "bad". These rules have been implied with most religions on Earth.

The stage was set to control all who believe in this institution. Corrupt ones covered up the truth. When you believe in yourself, this allows your Light to shine for you to explore, grow, and Love.

A God, religion, or place will not do this for you.

You are an eternal Soul. You are here to experience joy and Love.

There is no good or bad. Simply experiences that lead you down one road or another. A bible was written long ago, communicating ways of Being with Love and compassion. Many of these writings were either destroyed, manipulated, or changed into deceiving the masses.

The manipulated versions that have been put forward states there is but one god to look up to and place this belief in a constitution called the church.

There is not simply one god, a male god, or one of a particular gender.

We know with these words and knowledge there will be arising. We say to those who are deeply ingrained in the church to go within. Does this resonate with your heart that there would only be one god and that this god is a man? It is equal between a man and a woman. The Divine Feminine and the Divine Masculine.

There is Source, a Supreme Consciousness, that is for all Universes.

Source is Love, Pure Consciousness, and connected to all matter and life.

When one takes a look at the Vatican and goes to this illusion of worship, which we call a place of horror and deceit, ask yourself the question of why is there gold in this institution when people are starving and there is poverty in the streets? Why is there an imbalance and the churches continue to ask for money when people are struggling to get by?

Yes, some churches will take care of others and feed the

poor and shelter the homeless, however, it is with the intent that those they help will be "saved" and at what cost?

There is no saving to be done. Each Soul is pure Love at its core.

Jeshua and Mary Magdalene both said this through their teachings. It is the deceit that manipulated the information that Mary Magdalene was a prostitute and Jeshua was the almighty one. It was together, the support of each other and the Love of one another that they created the purest, heartfelt teachings to all. Once their voices were heard and people began to feel this in their hearts, there was the plan to take out Jeshua himself in the most harmful and crucifying way. This way was to teach others that yes if you follow this path, look at what awaits you.

With Mary Magdalene, it was easy to put a reward out for her death and begin to place rumors around her so-called infidelities. Mary Magdalene was able to escape and find a way to continue with her teachings of Love and compassion. With whatever humans believe in, we say that it is wonderful to believe in something and to have faith in something.

Know that something is you. You are the answer that you've been waiting for. Not a church, religion, or priest saying you will be condemned or looked down upon if you do not believe in Christ or have not been baptized.

This will be the greatest undoing and the greatest cover-up that will be revealed. For centuries, churches have been a coverup for the horrors of sexual abuse to children and adults. Healing will take place for many once this intuition is dismantled.

Finances

The next outcome that will come forward on Earth is the dismantling of the Financial Institutions. Take a deeper look at how this was originally built, as this is within a pyramid scheme and structure.

Humanity places their hard-earned money into accounts making little interest and then pays high rates to borrow when needed. This may look like this is set up to protect the economy and laws at hand, but it is to control the individuals and masses into thinking this is the only way.

Throughout the universes, banks and money are a 3D version of control.

There is no need for money in other dimensions. For land, places and planets belong to all in the higher realms. Exchanges are done with services for one another and within many planets, there is no give and take.

The ultimate goal is to be of service to all. There will be a process of eliminating illusions within the banking systems on Earth. This will begin in 2022 as many awaken and move forward in the years to come. A lifting of the veil will show what was put in place to control humanity.

With the lifting of the veil, new ways will come to support no longer needing money and banks as they once were.

The banking industry will go through a complete overhaul, no longer serving the purpose to benefit the greed and monopoly of the banking corporations, and thus, the elite.

CEO's

CEOs around the world will no longer exist in their roles. It will come to humanity's realization of the unbalanced ways of pay for these individuals. There will come a rise from humanity to no longer allow money to be distributed in this way.

No longer will the rich be getting richer. Around the globe, people will see the distribution of their wealth in the coming years. For many that hold this wealth, they will be awakened to the imbalance that is plaguing Earth and work hard at disturbing their funds where it is needed the most.

As many awaken to the imbalances around the planet,

there will be peace among those that give away their wealth and freedom will come into their Souls.

For those that do not awaken and hold onto their wealth with greed and contempt, they will remain in the 3rd dimension along with the ongoing experiences for that individual.

Schools and Education

Throughout time on planets and universes, coming together, to learn and grow, have been about truth, wisdom, and expansion.

In the past few centuries, schooling on Earth has taken on a controlled environment where the student must follow the rules and regulations of the school and its teacher. The teacher is also given a curriculum to follow and teach to its students.

This way which has been taught over the centuries is another way to control society and bring trauma and pain into each Soul if they do not meet and follow the criteria at hand.

Each Soul is different, unique, and special. There are many ways for a Soul to learn and understand their differences and talents are one and the same.

In the years to come, learning and education will see an overhaul in the entire system. There will no longer be prestigious schools to get into with high tuition and fees. The hierarchy of schools will end.

With the energies coming in very strongly for 2021 and beyond, new enlightened ways of teaching will present themselves.

Meditation will begin every day at the beginning of younger school grade classes, along with mindfulness and movement throughout the day to release pent-up energies which allow learning to be kept fresh and new.

Schools will teach about energy, life, relationships, emotions, food, animals, and much more that attain to how each child will move forward in their life. There will be tests that examine what the child's unique gifts are. Later on, when they are an adolescent, they will decide where and how they would like to serve their community and planet. These tests are not to be feared or prepared for. They are done through insight and universal love that will enhance the Soul's path on their journey of Light. This will not be set in stone either, as the child has the right to move into any field of their choice down the road. There will be schools that will pertain to the child's field of choice and their education will be one of acceleration and excitement. There will no longer be anxiety with tests, learning, and being in a school.

Meditation will be taught at a young age and continue to be maintained throughout the school years and into one's daily routine as an adult. Meditation teaches self-regulation of the mind and breath. In turn, anxiety, depression, and the dread that is associated with schools, tests, and fitting into certain crowds will be eliminated. With all students meditating, there will be a greater expansion of Love and compassion.

There will also be options after adolescent learning which allows access for anyone around the world to learn at any school they desire from their own home. Online learning will look quite different than what it is today, as there will be technology that will be used where you feel like you're right there in the classroom. This technology will be used for children in their later years. This option will be available for all Souls to access the learning they desire no matter where they reside.

Teachers will be accountable for the way they teach as there will be a universal system set in place for the awakened ones to be in teaching roles.

The way teachers educate their students currently will not exist. There will no longer be teachers that do the bare minimum and do not have the students' best interests at heart. It is through experience and providing space to express one's own thoughts and gifts that learning on all levels of the Soul will take place.

Food Industry

There is currently a food monopoly on your planet. Ads, exchanges, and belief systems are set in place with human programming to convince humanity that you need meat, dairy, sugar, alcohol, and caffeine to enjoy life, stay awake or be healthy and strong.

As we mentioned before, there was a time on this planet when humans, animals, and all life coexisted in harmony, respect, and honor. Currently, the mainstream meat industry has no respect for living animals and the environment they are kept in.

No human needs dairy or meat to survive and thrive.

Fruits, vegetables, nuts, seeds, water, and sunlight help to keep your body thriving along with sleep, meditation, and movement. Once humanity moves into releasing its current belief systems on food, there will be a change in the health of the planet.

This will also occur as the density on the planet lifts as more humans awaken.

Accelerated Light is being moved into the planet and with that comes the change in each one of your bodies. There will be less need for meat and, for some, there will be repulsion with even thinking of eating meat ever again.

The "norm" will be reversed in the coming years with

less meat in society and a much lighter way of eating will be the way. When people do eat animals, there will be respect for its life and death.

Processed foods will be eliminated as well as alcohol and drugs.

Any Soul wanting to continue to experience these illusions will have the choice to stay in the 3rd dimension.

Animal "delicacies", parts of animals, fur, and skin for sale will no longer be permitted.

Countries, where animals are kept in cages for entertainment with cruel and unsanitary conditions, will be condemned and no longer tolerated.

This shift will happen very quickly, along with no more breeding for the perfect animal, pets for-profit, or a certain status in society.

Governments

Within the governed laws of society where you live, it was made to believe that the ones you vote in would be for the people and with the people. Behind the scenes, many of the ones you have voted in to govern your laws have been manipulated and coerced into playing the game. Sometimes these elected individuals are caught, however, most of the time the public is not made aware of what is truly happening.

The people who currently make the laws and decisions spend the taxpayer's money to their advantage and to the 3D way of life. They have not consulted the public on major decisions that would affect all and the planet.

What will now come into play is the breakdown of the ones that govern your laws. There will no longer be politics, candidates, and the astronomical amount of money that is spent in these endeavors.

There will be councils that are different from the ones that currently exist. These councils will be for the entire planet and smaller ones will coexist for the areas you live in. With the Light energy that is coming in, there will no longer be payments, bribes, cheating, bullying, and lying in these groups and to humanity as a whole.

The councils that will be formed are governed by peace, goodwill, and service to all.

Many are wondering how this is possible, for decades humanity has gone along with voting for a party or an individual. This will no longer be necessary, for what we want all to know is, the energy will be different. It will be of a higher dimension, the ways and laws of governing previously will not work in the coming years.

The dismantling of the government will be a natural process.

Yes, this will take time and will not happen overnight. This will not take decades to be implemented. This is happening within this decade that you are currently in.

Healthcare

The healthcare system on your planet is an outdated systematic way. There will be technologies that will come forward with vibration and sound tools to help heal the body. There will be technology pods that can heal bones and perform surgery for each person without opening the body.

PharmaCare will no longer exist. The medicines and drugs that are prescribed to humans now are ones to make you sick and implement harm to the body. Yes, some of these drugs will prolong your life a bit longer but at what cost?

Many people are set in their ways in this belief system that the doctor knows best. They must take the prescriptions they have been given. To this we say, look at the situation with opioids. PharmaCare and the people behind the scenes knew exactly what this would do to society and the afflicting harm of addiction on Souls and their loved ones.

Do your own research and see what is happening at hand. Sarah, our channeler, discovered through her body's signs that her iron was low. She went to see her doctor and was prescribed iron pills with a list of ones to take. With Sarah's research, each one of the iron pills that were prescribed had cancer-causing ingredients in each brand. There were over four different brands that were recommended.

Sarah's intuition led her to a vegan blood-booster to help her. When the doctor called back a few weeks later to see how she was doing, she let the doctor know she did not take any of the recommended pills for the ingredients would cause harm to her body. Sarah mentioned what she was taking instead and the doctor asked for the name so they could then prescribe that brand to their other patients that had the same issue.

The health technologies that will be used on Earth for its inhabitants are technologies that will be downloaded into Souls that have awakened and channeled Light technology information from other Realms. This Light technology has been used for millions of years throughout the galaxies.

There will also be a simpler, more holistic way to healthcare. Energy Healers, Sound Therapists, and specialized Souls will have the ability to scan the body and see what ails you, this will be the new norm.

Hospitals will no longer be needed as these pods will be sufficient for all diagnoses.

There will be farmers that will grow herbs and plants to holistically and naturally keep the body well.

There will be healers in food and medicine that will be able to prescribe different tonics, teas, plants, and roots to help those in need.

The way forward is in harmony with the planet and, in turn, in harmony with your mind, body, and Soul. This is what creates optimal health, well-being, and community.

Natural Resources

Currently, Mother Earth's natural resources are being taken from her at such a velocity that leaves one's head spinning.

Over the next ten years, all mining, drilling and seeking oil, metals, and other resources from the depths of this planet will cease. This will include the destruction of forests and taking away the natural habitat of the animals.

Once humans come to terms with the destruction that has taken place on Earth, there will be a collective decision on how to move forward. Reversing the irreparable damage that has been done.

There will be no use for products such as plastic and other harmful packaging that are currently being used.

Holidays and gift-giving will also change. There will no longer be the material overwhelm that it is now. It is about the time and experience with one another that is to be loved and cherished.

For as life continues, each Soul will awaken to what makes one feel better, is with fewer material items. All will awaken to see how harmful it is to produce plastics and other materials that do not biologically break down and pollute the Earth.

Yes, humanity and Mother Earth are now at the tipping point. It will take every human to do their part for change and become aware of one's habits. The Light will continue to enter each human and will help to increase your awareness in every crevice of your Being.

MEMORIES

As each human awakens to their Divine Essence, memories will be remembered from long ago. This is important to know, as your memories hold pieces of information to help you in this current lifetime.

These memories will naturally begin to reveal themselves over the coming years. They have always been with you, however, when incarnating on this planet, they were kept hidden. Each Soul knows this is what happens before you enter the Earth plane.

Within each of your memories is the key to advancement and to know every aspect of yourself which, in turn, is the understanding of the collective as a whole.

This concept may be hard to grasp. Please know that overall we are all connected and One. Previously this was touched upon, as we all come from Source, Light consciousness.

There are multiple lives which are aspects of yourself that are happening simultaneously. In dream time, you can tap into one of your existing lives and bring that memory forth.

As each Soul's memories come forward, there is an integration in the body and mind which needs to take place. You may become very tired and feel the need to rest. Trust this process of memory allocation and the Divine timing when this happens for you.

Each Soul reading this will have this experience and we advise you to write down the dreams that come through and the memories that came forth. Ask your Highest Self and your Team for the messages in dreams. Each dream will have an underlying message that may not be able to be determined in the actual dream itself.

TRANSITIONS

There will be many transitions that take place over the coming years. This is on an individual, society, and planetary level. Through the layers of transition comes awareness, awakening, and expansion. Honor each transition that you go through on a Soul level, as a society and planetary level, for it is important to know how far you have come and how much you have accomplished in a very short amount of time.

Individual

Each individual will go through a process of growth in their emotional, mental, and spiritual bodies as each Soul awakens.

As the Light energy begins to move at an accelerated rate through your planet, this will shift as each one of you goes through leaps and bounds in Soul growth.

Each individual will go through many experiences at a rapid pace to achieve moving into the 5th dimension. This will only apply to the Souls that want to be part of the 5th and higher dimensions.

As we have mentioned before, each Soul has a choice. The Souls that are choosing to depart now, honor them for the choices they have made and the Light they were able to share with each one of you.

Society

As a society, there will be balance and moderation. The awakening has already begun, shifting the awareness between the poor and rich. As each Soul undergoes its own awakening, so too will the privileged give away their funds to create an equal playing field for all.

All Souls will be treated equally and there will be no hierarchy in society any longer. Monarchies and the wealthy will cease and be dissolved into an awakening of their own. They will come out of their bubble and see their illusion for what it truly was.

Planetary

The planetary transition will be a large one.

There will no longer be a division between countries.

There will no longer be borders that separate one country from one another. These borders will be eliminated in the years to come among states, provinces and nations.

Your planet will be guided as a whole among all that live there. How is this possible? How will this work?

As the awakening occurs, there is a shift in all energies. There is no support to hold the old ways with the 3D density.

Going forward there is lightness, love, and community. The majority that reside here on Earth are here for the larger purpose to awaken and help each other ascend.

As we have mentioned before, there will be communities all around the world. Within these communities is a council which is not like the councils that are currently set up in your societies.

These councils are for the greater good, with the utmost highest intentions for the highest good of all.

These councils will then interact with the planetary council, helping not only the planet as a living Being but all that live here.

The border walls will come down, maps will be drawn anew and there will be new names for the lands on your planet as the energy continues to shift.

Within each community, there will be temples that rise again. These temples are for healing, Soul growth, teaching, and ascension.

Schools of trade will be within each community, and there will be other schools for specific training that will exist all around the globe. Each Soul will no longer need planes to get them to these schools. The technology will be advanced enough for humans to learn from home if the Soul desires to learn from that school.

As we have said before, travel will not be necessary, for one will appreciate where they live and will be able to communicate with anyone they would like to, no matter the distance.

ENERGETIC TIMELINES

Each Soul has timelines in their current life to accomplish and experience certain goals that were originally in their Soul contract.

Due to the intensity of the Light coming in, starting from the December Solstice in 2020, many timelines are shifting and are no longer set in stone.

Each Soul will achieve their goals within their contracts at a much quicker pace.

There was a time on this planet that many of us Light Beings were waiting in anticipation to see if the scales would tip in the Light's favor once again. Many timelines could have occurred if the mass of the Lightworkers had not maintained their Light and frequency.

This was accomplished and now there is a quickening,

a righting of the ways.

Within each of your timelines, there will be freedom in the Soul and peace in your Being, for no ill harm will come to you in this Now timeline. For many of you in your past lifetimes, trauma was experienced in your death when you left your physical body. When speaking your truth, helping others, and walking your path, some sought to silence you.

Many were burned at the stake, killed, and tortured. Once again, we want to make this clear to you, you are now safe to walk your path, speak your truth and raise your voices for others when there is wrongdoing.

There is no longer the threat of physical harm as there once was in your past lives.

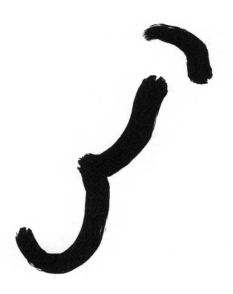

WHAT IS MY PURPOSE?

Many of you may wonder what your purpose is. How do you begin?

For those of you who are reading this now, your curiosity, what excites you and lights you up, will move you into your purpose. Trust that you will know your purpose in time and enjoy the stepping stones that lead you down the path.

There will also be many Souls that will become teachers. Not in the traditional sense of teaching as educators.

This will be one of higher purpose, with teachings of oneness and the ability to wake within each Soul their abilities, their power, and their innate strength of wisdom and courage moving forward. There are the right amount of teachers now on your planet that will be guided forward to help those in their communities and around the world. This is not coming from a place of ego where one will become famous with their teachings and be known all around the globe.

Your teachings will come forward with your partnership with Spirit and the acknowledgment of such.

There will be many teachers needed as there are billions of Souls living on your planet. Each Soul will seek out a new teacher at different times in their growth.

For some of you, you will teach in smaller groups and for others, you will teach in one-on-one sessions.

There are a few that will teach in larger groups. These Souls are awakened now and are acquiring large amounts of knowledge from their past lives and the support of many Light Beings to help them awaken their gifts when they are ready.

It will be an honor for each teacher to share their wisdom. There is also the acknowledgment of the bravery and courage it takes for each Soul to seek out a teacher as one continues to grow on their path. This is recognized within one another.

Each Soul that seeks out a teacher is trusting that individual on an energetic level.

This will take some time for some Souls to trust another. For it has been centuries that many have learned to not trust, as they have been betrayed and hurt in the past. The way of not trusting will no longer exist in the 5th dimension.

That is why many Souls are now beginning to have faith in their energy and listen to what their intuition is communicating to their body, mind, and Spirit. You are all learning a new way of life.

PLANETARY CHANGES

As your planet moves into a higher frequency, there will be planetary changes as the Earth ascends. Yes, the Earth herself will heat up and the elements will adjust with these changes accordingly. There will be shifts in the seasons and they will not be the same as they once were. Some seasons will shorten in length and others will increase.

As each Soul awakens, there is the realization that nothing stays the same. Energy is fluid and in constant movement. Thus with the adjustment in seasons, this will not be upsetting to any awakened Soul as there is awareness to accept the changes at hand.

As the Light continues to increase on your planet, there will be a stronger bond in the community. The communities that will form and unite in Love and service will help each other as ocean waters rise, lands separate and rise.

Once communities and technologies come together to unite the health of the planet, that is when the tides will turn for more stabilization on Earth.

Each Soul has a part to play. Before you came into your human form, you knew what had to be done, experienced, and learned. This is not about passing the responsibility to the younger generations either. Each Soul can do something now to help raise the vibration and frequency thus bringing awareness to the masses to help in their ascension.

WHAT CAN I DO?

No matter your age, one can always go within.

Find out who you are and work on the layers that need to be released, healed, and forgiven in all aspects of the Soul. The blinders are coming off in this lifetime and there will be no more going back to sleep for any awakened Soul. The time is here to use, trust and move with your intuition. Each one of you reading this will have a variety of pathways that will flow into your purpose and awakening. Each Soul will continue to have epiphanies and awakenings throughout its lifetime.

Your life is a dance of energy, learning, and growth.

When you can let go of beliefs and ideas that hold you back, this can bring in more happiness to oneself.

Each of your journeys will be different.

Trauma, families, friends, work, school, and many varied elements will create experiences for you to go through. Each Soul will acquire a greater understanding of the bigger picture with the energy that has now come into your planet.

As your understanding awakens, trust your intuition. Your insights will lead you to what you need to know for your next step.

If one misses an opportunity, the road might steer in another direction to get you to the same experience or an even better one.

Our point is that there is not a set of rules that comes with your life. You have all you need right here and right now. It is trusting your energy, YOU, your heart, will lead you to where you need to go.

Each Soul that is here on the planet is needed for this evolutionary shift. Each one of you has gifts, ideas, and abilities that are needed for the collective.

This is the biggest shift this planet has ever seen. To move through dimensions to a higher frequency while in a physical vessel. This is Ascension.

Currently, all parts of the human are now being affected, physically, emotionally, mentally, and spiritually as this shift occurs.

For it is not only this life that you're living in that is being affected. It is all of your lifetimes on Earth and other planets that are coming forward for releasing, healing and forgiveness.

As healing takes place emotionally and mentally, it is very important to ground your energies into the Earth. Mother Earth and nature will naturally help reset your energies and bring calmness into your Being while this is occurring.

If you feel alone, we recommend adopting an animal that you can care for. Many animals are in need of love, care, and support. When loving and caring for an innocent animal, the amount of love that is returned to you is unconditional. Heart-felt purity is felt at your core.

Looking after an animal can ease the burden of what you're going through emotionally and mentally. Physically, it can get you outside more often if you adopt a dog or a cat if they like to go for walks.

The enormity of this transformation for each individual and Mother Earth is astronomical. It is being felt into the cosmos. Within this galaxy, there are ripple effects that affect each planet and Soul on this energetic plane.

As the structures of religion begin to unravel, many Souls will realize that unconditional love does not put restrictions on the way you love or who you love as a Soul. It does not matter if you love a woman, a man, or another Being. It is the heart, the energy inside the Soul that one will be drawn to like a magnet.

This is the way forward for all Souls in the 5th dimension and beyond. No restrictions on who you love within any religious or government structure. This will be a great unraveling in the years to come.

Religions have had the biggest impact on the 3rd dimension. To be able to control a Soul while making them feel like something is wrong with them if they don't love a certain way or live a certain way within a set amount of rules is quite a feat.

This has been accomplished for many centuries and yet some Souls did not follow these rules. Many years ago, many females walked the Earth with great insight and healing abilities. Time and time again, these brave Souls were condemned for practicing the ways of the Land, healing others, and providing support to their communities. Many were outcasts and looked down upon as they did not fit the "rules".

Some of these females were labeled as witches and were either burned, hung, or beaten to death for having helped others. They were targeted by ones that held false power.

For many women, these past lives are coming forward to be healed and joined with this current life.

For many reading these words, they will feel this in their Soul and will instantly remember remedies or how to place their hands on a tree, animal, or another Soul for healing. This healing can also be through telepathy, support, holding space, and with the intention to heal.

Many people will remember ways to open portals for energy work, planetary grids, and open access points to other dimensions for healing. This takes skill and an awareness of what one is doing. There will be Teams of Support that will come in for each individual that is drawn to healing in this way.

The men and women that condemned these Souls long ago will also walk the Earth again for a chance to reverse the karma and bring healing forward to their Soul. There are valuable lessons in each lifetime that a Soul goes through. This will be reviewed once crossing over and joining with your Highest Self.

THE HUMANS ROLE

Each human has a role to play in the years to come. Now is the time for integration. Integrating the energies that are coming into your human vessel and realigning to the truth as the veil is lifted. The veil of forgetfulness.

Within your role comes clarity. The clarity to love fully with no strings attached, no conditions, and being able to love without fear. There will be an equal balance between all colors of skin and genders. You are all human and as one species will work together as a whole for the well-being of all who live here on your planet. The realization for all moving into the 5th dimension is that we all come from the same Source. There is no separation.

HUMAN NEEDS

Humans have many needs that require tending to.

Humans currently require water, food, clothing, shelter, and money to survive.

For each body and each vessel, it is the awareness of what goes in and on the body which is important. It takes time to care for the body each day, to nourish it with clean water, nutritious food, and to allow the body to move daily. This awareness comes in more so as the energy shifts, more humans awaken and their bodies require this awareness.

One of the biggest changes coming will be the exchange of money. Physical money will be no longer.

In its place will be exchanges for goods and a digital system. All humans will receive a basic amount for their needs and this will be all that is needed. The materialistic way of consuming will be over. The excess will be no more.

For some humans, this will cause panic inside of them. For when they purchase items, this can cause a temporary high in their brains until they face their reality again. This is a false sense of feeling well. This false feeling of consumption will not exist in the energy that the majority of humans and your planet are moving into.

This is what we want all to know, the ones that have set up the systems are now crumbling. There are other ways in the financial, education, health, and community systems that are beneficial to all. The current systems in place that humans are using are based on a hierarchical system. The rich keep getting richer and the poor keep getting poor.

All Beings are equal. This false reality currently in place will diminish.

Each human needs to know that their basic needs will be looked after. Imagine, for so many when this happens, what will be accomplished. From a collective standpoint, looking at your world where every human is taken care of, you begin to look at your world with a fresh pair of eyes, one of hope and renewal.

MONEY ATTACHMENTS, MINDSET & SEPARATION

Currently, many Souls have obtained the mentality to work hard so then they can go on vacation and play.

People cling to how much money is in their bank accounts, homes, cars, and pensions.

This is not your true worth. As each human releases their holds on false attachments with their money and materials, this opens a flow, a higher frequency of greater awareness. It is through the attachments that one holds onto the 3D way of life and controls.

Each human will go through releasing this mindset, as

the energy becomes stronger and stronger. No Soul that is destined to move into the 5th dimension will want to remain in the old ways as it will feel heavy. It can be difficult and challenging to be in as the separation of the dimensions continues. There will also be a separation from family and friends for many. This is not an upsetting ordeal.

Your energy will not want to be around others that are not compatible with your frequency. You may still have threads to family, however, over time you may organically separate. Yes, you can still have contact with your family members and friends from the past, however, you will be aligned to other Souls who are more of an energetic match.

There will be many Souls that will leave the planet over the next ten years. This is not to cause alarm or upset one's Soul. The Soul's that are leaving have finished their contracts and reached their goals.

The Souls that are here on Earth in the next ten to twenty years have come to be part of the change within Earth and humanity.

SOUL PHASES

There are phases within your Soul as each one of you progresses to the 5th dimension.

Here is a condensed list of what your Soul will experience:

Phase One: *Awakening*

The veil begins to lift. Your Soul goes through the awakening process. Phase One can be a shock to your entire system. There can be many physical sensations in this part of your awakening. This takes time for the body, mind, and Spirit to adjust to. There are also levels within your awakening. After the initial wake-up call, it can take years for the layers of conditioning from society to be released as there is continuous work that one must do to move into the next phase. Part of the work we speak of is bringing the ego back into balance with your Soul by first releasing the ego and the death of the ego. The other layers that are released are the traumas and memories of your past lives on Earth. Place no time limit on Phase One as this is in your Soul contract. Know once you awaken there is no turning back to the sleeping state. There will be times when your Soul and energy will be tired with the relentless work of releasing the layers, do not give up. There will always be help around you to aid you through this phase.

Phase Two: *Integration*

Information, past lives, memories, and dreams all become activated. There are layers within your integration. Physically, there can be many sensations throughout your body when your integration occurs. Rest, self-care, grounding, and trust are what is needed during this time. During this phase, many gifts that you once had will be revealed. This is a time to be proactive with practicing your gifts and dedicating your energy to prepare for your mission or purpose.

Phase Three: *Completion*

You move fully into the role of your mission. There can be parts of your mission that are activated before your whole mission is complete. The final result is a smoother path ahead and this is from the hard work that you've done on yourself. You are now ready to be of service to humanity.

MOVEMENT THROUGH THE PHASES

As each Soul moves through the first two phases, emotions can arise.

It is an unsettling feeling to be controlled and

manipulated into a certain way of life.

It has been years, even centuries that this has been going on.

It was during the first world war that manipulation tactics began. This was with the radio being kept at a certain frequency to keep the minds locked at a vibration and level of control.

Later on the food, air and water were affected.

The television has continual messages in the frequency and flashes on the screen that are meant to numb and sedate people. If you look at its content, the news is based on continual fear being played over and over again. There are addictive programs such as game shows, crime, comedy, and many others. Ask yourself the question: do any of these shows lift me up? Do they make me laugh and keep my vibration high? Each program that is broadcast has the intention for a level of addiction to occur within each individual.

Similar to the corporations which knew about opioids and created them to cause harm to humans, so does television and its programming.

When a Soul is completely awake, it can look back at the level in all facets of life, and of the level of control these Beings have put on this planet. We say had because that is now changing very quickly to past tense.

Humanity's Guidebook to Ascension

FINAL NOTES

Take the time to absorb the information that has been laid out before you and go back throughout the book as many times as you need.

Even though your species is moving into an accelerated state of energy, this is the time to work on oneself.

This is the first step and a crucial one to your process. Without taking the time and diving deep into releasing and clearing the layers of conditions brought onto you by society, the detachment of your false reality can be a much harder and longer road.

The next two books are about the freedom that each one of you has in your Light. These stories hold memories of your past lives, other realms, and planets that come forward to help in your ascension on Earth. *Please be forewarned we highly recommend absorbing only one to two chapters at a time in books two and three. These books are not 3D books, where you can read in one sitting. Books two and three are potent and are meant to have time in between the chapters to provide your energy to heal, clear, and adjust to the frequency.*

We thank you for taking the time to read this information and the books to follow.

It is an honor to be able to help with our contribution to humanity and Mother Earth's ascension.

We are the Divine Light Collective.

GRATITUDE

To the reader,

Thank you for purchasing this book! I hope there is some insight, tool, or Divine wisdom that will help make your life a bit easier on your ascension path. Moving into the 5th dimension is a hard, tough road.

However, once the layers are released, cleared and the many veils are dissolved there is another reality that exists.

There is wonderment in your life, every day. Your mind is released from the shackles of the 3D, bringing freedom to your Soul.

It's a whole new beginning...

Wishing you all the very best on your journey into the 5th dimension.

Love and Light to all,

Sarah A'ryana

With deep gratitude in my heart, I thank the Divine Light Collective for this opportunity to channel these writings for humanity. In March of 2020 when we first connected I was on board and excited for this connection. Little did I know that channeling this information would also include many more awakenings, Soul growth, and a deep letting go process of the 3D realm as I continued to move forward into my Earth mission. It truly is an honor to have worked with you all.

To my Soul Sister Deborah, this book would not be what it is today without your insights, patience, and incredible design. Thank you for your beautiful photographs as they provide an additional element of healing for all to enjoy. You are a 5D artist who is ahead of our time! It is a privilege to have you in my life.

Angel Light
Photo by Sarah A'ryana 2020

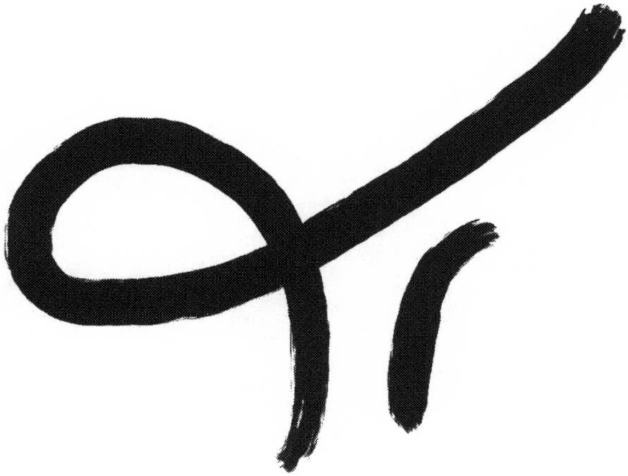

A NOTE ABOUT THE AUTHOR

Sarah A'ryana is a Lightworker that heard the call from Mother Earth to help in humanity's Ascension.

Through writing, channeling, healing and teaching, Sarah is fulfilling her life's purpose and Soul mission.

Sarah lives on Vancouver Island, Canada with her family and loves to connect daily with nature and the beauty of this world.

For more information, visit saraharyana.com

A NOTE ABOUT THE ARTIST

Tartaruga Feliz is an artist, healer and Freedom seeking Soul who happily designed this book and took the pictures that accompany it. Born in Brazil and assembled in Germany, her work brings a mix of Art and technology, with a focus on Character Design and spreading Kindness to humanity.

Moved by intuitive guidance and collaborating with many collectives of Light Beings surrounding the Earth and beyond, Tartaruga Feliz has participated in numerous exhibitions collectively and individually around the world.

For more information, visit tartarugafeliz.com

ILLUSTRATIONS

DISCLAIMER

Please note: All views in this book are from the Divine Light Collective. Please use your own discernment regarding the health and well-being of your mind, body and Soul with making decisions for yourself based on what you read in this book.

The information in this book is for education purposes only. It is presented as a guideline to aid your energy into the 5th dimension. If you wish to implement the ideas from this book in your life, you are taking full responsibility for your actions. Consult with your physician for your individual needs.

Made in United States
Troutdale, OR
11/11/2023

14476329R00186